ALSO BY JOSIAH BUNTING III

Ulysses S. Grant: The American Presidents Series

All Loves Excelling

An Education for Our Time

The Lionheads

The
MAKING
of a
LEADER

Chief of Staff George Catlett Marshall Jr.
in a photograph that appeared on the cover
of *TIME* magazine on July 29, 1940

The

MAKING

of a

LEADER

· · ·

The Formative Years of
George C. Marshall

Josiah Bunting III

Alfred A. Knopf
New York
2024

THIS IS A BORZOI BOOK
PUBLISHED BY ALFRED A. KNOPF

Copyright © 2024 by Josiah Bunting III

All rights reserved. Published in the United States by Alfred A.
Knopf, a division of Penguin Random House LLC, New York,
and distributed in Canada by Random House of Canada, a
division of Penguin Random House Canada Limited, Toronto.

www.aaknopf.com

Knopf, Borzoi Books, and the colophon are registered
trademarks of Penguin Random House LLC.

Frontispiece: Farm Security Administration—Office of War
Information Photograph Collection, Library of Congress

Library of Congress Cataloging-in-Publication Data
Names: Bunting, Josiah, III, [date] author.
Title: The making of a leader : the formative years
of George C. Marshall / Josiah Bunting III.
Description: First United States edition. |
New York : Alfred A. Knopf, 2024.
Identifiers: LCCN 2023004371 (print) | LCCN 2023004372 (ebook) |
ISBN 9781400042586 (hardcover) | ISBN 9780385350426 (ebook)
Subjects: LCSH: Marshall, George C. (George Catlett),
1880–1959—Military leadership. | Generals—United States—
Biography. | United States. Army—Biography. | Statesmen—
United States—Biography. | Leadership—United States—Case
studies. | United States—History, Military—20th century.
Classification: LCC E745.M37 B86 2024 (print) |
LCC E745.M37 (ebook) | DDC 973.918092 B—dc23
LC record available at https://lccn.loc.gov/2023004371
LC ebook record available at https://lccn.loc.gov/2023004372

Jacket photograph: Lt. George C. Marshall (detail), c.1907. Courtesy
of the George C. Marshall Foundation, Lexington, Virginia.
Jacket design by Ariel Harari

Manufactured in the United States of America
First Edition

In memory of

Herbert Nash Dillard,

teacher, mentor, and great friend

Contents

Marshall and Me

A relatively controversial boarding school career surely foreclosed any possibility of my admission to a respected college on the Eastern Seaboard. So, to the marines I went. During my two-year stint in the corps, I had a friendly encounter with a young marine officer in the Mediterranean. Amid our practice of amphibious landings on the coasts of Libya, Italy, Greece, and the like, this officer one day asked me whether I had "ever heard of the Virginia Military Institute."

"Heard of it," I remember saying. "You should think I'm going there."

By some stroke of luck or providence, I was admitted to the institute, thus becoming a "rat," the term used to describe first-year students at VMI.

About a week after I arrived at VMI, an announcement had been made in the barracks that all members of the fourth class—freshmen—were to report to Jackson Memorial Hall to hear from an important guest speaker.

Walking to VMI's major assembly venue, I noted the beauty of the late-summer day, curious as to why we were being called to Jackson Memorial Hall. Once I found my seat in the front row, the marine two-star superintendent of VMI, General George R. E. Shell, introduced a distinguished alumnus to the class now assembled: Frank McCarthy.

A veteran of the Second World War, this alumnus had served throughout the war as a senior aide to General George Catlett Marshall Jr. The occasion for this visit was Marshall's death, in Washington, three days earlier. After briefly reviewing Marshall's military career, his subsequent service as secretary of state, and many of his accolades, including a Nobel Peace Prize, I noticed a change in the speaker's voice.

Plainly overcome by the demands of his mission to deliver the news of Marshall's death, McCarthy was led off the stage by General Shell. This remains the most vivid memory of my cadetship at VMI, and it was, I suppose, the germ of a lifelong interest in George Catlett Marshall.

"Some things don't happen in novels, only in life," a wise man once said.

Josiah Bunting III
Newport, Rhode Island

Formation and Biography

George C. Marshall lived a life of truly distinguished service to his country and the world. Every major historical treatment of World War II invariably discusses his role in subduing the totalitarian dictators of Europe. Nonspecialists and specialists alike, however, have perhaps most memorably encountered Marshall through the plan that bears his name, one that helped to define the postwar history of the European continent. In a time when new European conflicts threaten the robust social, political, and economic foundations for liberal democracy that the Marshall Plan hoped to provide, returning anew to the life of a figure so integral to twentieth-century global history seems quite appropriate.

Aside from the timeliness of a new Marshall biography, of which there are many, this book sets out a new program for attempting to understand the man who not only had many battlefield victories but who also came to be recognized for his contributions to world peace with a Nobel Prize. The seeming opposition of these two features of Marshall's life is but one of many unique facets of this ever-inimitable figure. Indeed, because historical consciousness of Marshall almost exclusively surrounds his leadership during and after World War II, many previous biographical treatments of Marshall have attempted to quickly illuminate his early years in anticipation of more extensively discussing his later contributions to (post)war efforts. The dual commitments of Marshall's other biographers—on the one hand, to briefly point readers' attention toward otherwise unknown stories of his early years, and on the other, to help readers appreciate the extent of Marshall's subsequent military and organizational prowess—have often prompted his biographers to focus more on the latter task than the former.

While the many full-length biographies of Marshall currently available do enlighten our understanding of this complex figure, they have yet to do justice to the near-providential personal and professional formation that made Marshall the man he would be on the eve of the Second World War. This biography of George Catlett Marshall thus does not relitigate or merely recapitulate what has already been written of his major World War II–era successes, nor does it commit the error of glossing over his formative years in anticipation of what a general reading audience seems to be most interested in: the demise of totalitarianism at the hands of the United States and its allies.

In attempting to provide today's reader an intimate and insightful account of how Marshall became the man who would play a major part in leading the United States through World War II, this biography retells the story of Marshall's formative years. In so doing, this biography hopes to make the generally interested and expert reader alike more familiar with the major people, events, and experiences that made Marshall distinguished not only in military skill but also in leadership of everyday men and women, of soldiers for democracy. In this way, a biography of Marshall's early years certainly will make the knowledgeable reader more attuned to the reasons for his subsequent successes, but it will also help those who have perhaps only briefly encountered Marshall appreciate why formation is such an integral part of making a leader—military and otherwise.

This biography of Marshall's formative years concludes on the eve of the conflict that would most shape popular memories of Marshall, as well as the course of world history. In the final pages of this story, the skills of mind and habit, the experiences of military engagement and peacetime, and the understanding of American soldiers for democracy coalesce in the now-experienced George Catlett Marshall. By a happy confluence of serendipity and professional calculation, however, Marshall's greatest contribution to the success of American arms in the Second World War was not his own tactical genius. Rather, his greatest contribution—a consequence of the character of an extraordinary and extended period of preparation—was in those whom he trained. Indeed, this pre–World War II period was one that introduced a large cohort of talented younger officers to Marshall, whom the soon-to-be chief of staff of the US Army, by unerring instinct and acute professional judgment, had long since identified as leaders of promise perfectly suited to the larger military and strategic challenges in the nation's future. A list of these men and their achievements in the Second World War is a list of matchless talent in full bloom. This contribution to the Allies' victory, alongside the quality of Marshall's political and strategic counsel to President Franklin D. Roosevelt, was this great soldier's largest wartime gift to his country.

In the fullness of time, it is richly ironic that this most distinguished of American soldiers was tendered his highest accolade in Oslo, years later, in recognition of an achievement even more sublime: the Nobel Peace Prize (conferred upon him as the author of the plan that bears his name). Designed to rehabilitate the social, cultural, political, and economic environment of Europe after World War II, it was this plan, the Marshall Plan, for which George Marshall is most remembered.

Introduced in a June 1947 speech at Harvard University, the Marshall Plan reminds us of the distinguished life lived by this distinguished general. Unlike many American military leaders today, Marshall did not flock to award ceremonies or boast on his public attire the many military marks to which he was certainly entitled. Instead, he embraced the opportunity to do as his country needed: first, in winning the Second World War, and later, in helping to ensure that the Allied victory enabled by the United States would not be destroyed at the hands of severe economic depression. Both of these responsibilities earned him much admirable recognition, but it is evidently not the *recognition* that Marshall had sought.

Though Marshall's leadership would be tested in theaters far from Pennsylvania and Virginia, where he was raised and first educated, it was undoubtedly shaped by the formation—the pedagogy of experience—with which Marshall had been infected since his boyhood. Indeed, it should be said that this was the best type of infection, one that sharpened Marshall's mind, skills, and personality. It was one that would make the man we now remember with such great reverence the leader we most needed.

The

MAKING

of a

LEADER

Chapter One

My Youngest and My Last

Although he was one of four children, and the youngest among them, George Catlett Marshall Jr. was raised essentially as an only child. The first of his brothers had died in infancy, and the second, Stuart Bradford Marshall, born in 1875, and almost six years George's senior, kept his distance. Chronology, temperament, and family chemistry isolated the surviving brothers from each other all their lives. There was a sister, Marie, four years older than George. They became attached to each other, as brother and sister normally do—but only after both had passed through adolescence. Thus, while Stuart and Marie were at school and his father at work, building a prosperous business in the manufacture of coke ovens, George Marshall had his mother to himself. A handsome woman of placid disposition and a sensibility amused rather than exasperated by childish misbehavior, she was the sustaining influence on Marshall's early life. A later age might have called her nonjudgmental;

the later age would have been wrong. Laura Marshall embodied rather than asserted the things she thought important. She was the strength of the family.

Stuart bore the full freight of his ambitious father's expectations. He bore them successfully, in school particularly, where early success always gratifies an ambitious parent. He was well-behaved and guarded his own turf with vigilance. Some years later, about the time Stuart was graduating from the Virginia Military Institute (VMI), George overheard him pleading with their mother: do not allow George to follow me to VMI. The imputation was that George, slow in his academic work, would disgrace the Marshall name. Family records disclose no expression of affection or act of fraternal solicitude between them.

Marshall's parents had been settled in Uniontown, Pennsylvania, for six years when George Catlett Marshall Jr. was born on the last day of 1880. It was a bustling village of about three thousand, and still, in the days before automobiles, sufficiently remote from Pittsburgh not to have been drawn into the ambit of the larger city. Though founded in the 1770s, it became an important waystation a generation later because of its proximity to the National Road, the early federal highway promoted by Thomas Jefferson. Eventually, this turnpike linked Cumberland, Maryland, with Vandalia, Illinois, and today, with a few S curves straightened out and several bridges replaced, is known as US Route 40.

The country near Uniontown is rich in colonial history. The first skirmishes of the French and Indian War occurred nearby, and the English general Edward Braddock, killed on his famous expedition to capture Fort Duquesne in 1755, is buried only a few miles from the town. George Washington's Fort Necessity, the scene of his early, if gallant, defeat (now rebuilt and moved a few miles), remains testimony to the area's strategic importance in the earliest years of western migration. As an adult, George Marshall Jr. was sometimes unable to conceal an irritated pride when his Virginian wife's family asserted the importance of their own heritage. He would not deny it, but he was uncomfortable with its corollary, not always unspoken: Albemarle County, Virginia.

In the years of Marshall's boyhood, Fayette County appeared a stage fitted out perfectly for the idyllic pursuits and pastimes of an unhurried age: a rich and gentle landscape of fresh green meadows, orchards, and forest; clotted rolling hills and two important crossecting rivers (the Monongahela and the Youghiogheny). The rivers and forests became the sometime habitat of George Marshall Sr. and his younger son, both devoted hunters and fishermen. All his life, George Marshall Jr. would be a lover of remote green places: they came to represent surcease, renewal, and, most of all, the healing balm of a remembered pleasure in his father's too-occasional companionship. The town itself, typical of the communities along the National Road, was quiet and amiable: this was

just before the beginning of contentious hyperactivity—
most of it rooted in the various labors connected with the
extraction of coal from the earth—that followed.

George's parents were conscious of their Southern
heritage and, in the case of Mr. Marshall, zealous in
asserting the importance of ancestry. A prosaic destiny
had led them out of Kentucky and into Pennsylvania;
they brought with them "the manners and morals of
their prewar youth."[1] (An American of the twenty-first
century must remind himself that prewar meant the
1840s and 1850s: pre–Civil War.)

Marshall Sr. watered these roots of ancestry ceaselessly, and with at least two consequences: first, that his
youngest son would grow into what his official biographer called "a species of Virginian," a man of dignity and
reserve; and second, that even before that slow transformation had begun, the adolescent Marshall was already
exasperated by what appeared to have been a long, arid
period in the family genealogy.[2] In a time and family
in which books were the common currency of evening
diversion (both father and mother read to their children),
a volume especially honored was W. M. Paxton's genealogy of the Marshall family. The boy learned its contents
thoroughly. His father's particular obsession was with
his collateral ancestor Chief Justice John Marshall (his
first cousin twice removed); and, less so, with another
kinsman, Robert E. Lee's brilliant aide, prominent at
Appomattox and possibly the author of Lee's *Farewell
Address to the Army of Northern Virginia,* Charles Mar-

shall. "It was about time for someone else to swim for the family," George Jr. decided.[3]

The younger George Marshall's father had participated in military action both farcical and tragic. He had grown to early manhood in Augusta, Kentucky, a locale described in the *New York Times* as "a gentle and pastoral land with a savage history. . . . [One of] rolling hills and fields in varying intense shades of green, limestone cliffs, red barns and blackened tobacco sheds."[4] At eighteen, in 1863, he served briefly with his own father—a member of the Home Guard of Augusta, Kentucky—commanded by a staunch Unionist, Dr. Joshua Bradford. With a few others they once rushed to the local wharf on the Ohio to warn Union gunboats that a large mounted Confederate detachment under Colonel Basil Duke was about to attack. The boats shoved off, firing an ineffectual volley for dignity's sake. White flags of surrender appeared in the windows of the houses along the river, the citizens either realizing they were ill prepared to fight off an attack or glad to welcome the Rebels. Not everyone saw the flags, however. Many who did not opened fire. Fire was returned.

When the engagement was over, thirty men lay dead, Confederate cavalrymen and Augusta citizens alike. The two Marshalls were captured by the Rebels, detained for a few days, then paroled, according to the practice of the day. They pledged their word not to take up arms again for the duration of the war. Here at the very border of a border state, such small actions and clumsy efforts to preserve honor or to defend one's town and kin or to intimidate enemies were common.

An unexpected consequence of the engagement was a partial repair of what had been an estrangement between Bradford's family and the Marshalls. Soon after the war ended, George Marshall married Bradford's niece, Laura. They then left Kentucky for Pennsylvania; again, a destiny less strange than ironic: the self-conscious heir to a resonant Virginia name leading his bride, via Kentucky, to Pennsylvania. Almost thirty years later, his son, George Catlett Marshall Jr. (to whom irony was an alien quality), would find himself explaining his Yankee accent to senior cadets at VMI.

Though its course has been anxiously scrutinized by two generations of scholars and historians, Marshall's childhood yields few definitive clues to his later eminence. He appears a puckish little brother: enterprising, active, forgetful. He was called "Flicker," a wheaten-haired boy with freckles and a pug nose. He conceived an early hatred of all schooling. There is a particularly vivid image of him, dating from 1885 or 1886, and still fresh in his own memory in the mid-1950s: he is being held to the side of a rocking chair, and his great-aunt Eliza Stuart is teaching him the Episcopal catechism and rudiments of arithmetic. From his vantage he can see his friends playing outside in the sun.

.   .   .

The Uniontown Marshalls lived in a two-story brick house on West Main Street, just at the edge of town. There was a large garden behind it—an arbor of pear trees, sycamores, and honey locusts. A clear shallow stream ran across the property, Coal Lick Run, the site of an early Marshall episode. With his best boyhood friend, Andy Thompson, George Jr. constructed a raft and offered ferry service across the stream, taking two or three girls aboard for the passage of ten feet. When the girls failed to produce the tickets George had printed, he flooded the vessel, causing it to sink midstream.

Just as the Marshall house lay at the edge of Uniontown, so too the town itself, barely seventeen miles north of the Mason-Dixon Line, subsisted at an edge, or rather limit, of a fading culture: the American Gilded Age, defined in popular memory as a languid drifting time of broad verandas, stout bewhiskered presidents, idle recreations, and spacious vistas. But the popular memory, however satisfying or sweet, remains dim. Crossecting currents, some still subterranean, had begun the remorseless work of transformation decades earlier. Uniontown was to be changed fundamentally over the next twenty years by the coal and coke industries. Among these early indicia were coke ovens in the nearby hill (many manufactured by Mr. Marshall and his partners), seen at night through gales of gaseous smoke. Soon, Uniontown began to attract immigrant laborers, hundreds of them, many who huddled near the town, living in boxcars, eking out a dreary subsistence living in the mines and factories nearby.

George C. Marshall Sr. appears as a kind of genteel Babbitt. He was tall, somewhat stout, sandy-haired, and gregarious. This George Marshall was a congenital joiner of clubs, an active Mason, a vestryman at Saint Peter's Episcopal Church, and a committed Democrat in a town and state warmly allegiant to the party of Abraham Lincoln and U. S. Grant. His younger son was christened at Saint Peter's in 1881 and would remain a nominal Episcopalian all his life. An early experience in the church, however, was not auspicious; it led to mild public humiliation, perhaps less embarrassing to the son than to the father. One Sunday morning, George Jr., tucked away behind the manual church organ (he had been retained to pump it for the hymns), had so immersed himself in reading a Nick Carter novel that he failed to note the end of the rector's sermon and the premonitory creaks and coughs signaling the expected beginning of the offertory hymn. The organist began to play, but the instrument emitted no sound. The boy's inattention was instantly known in Uniontown, and he was no longer chosen to pump the organ.

Nick Carter's adventure stories aside, Marshall also read the Frank Merriwell stories, then coming into fashion, and, soon after, the robust tales of the Victorian novelist G. A. Henty—a writer of historical fictions set in classical and medieval venues. In 1943, visiting the

ruins of ancient Carthage in Tunisia, Marshall told his
protégé Dwight D. Eisenhower that all he knew of Carthage and Hannibal he learned by reading Henty as a
boy. He also read Rudyard Kipling, and either read or
listened to someone read Sir Walter Scott (*Ivanhoe* was
his favorite), James Fenimore Cooper, Arthur Conan
Doyle, Charles Dickens, Ouida; and from historical
romances like *Don Orsino* and narratives like *History of
the Conquest of Mexico.* Much of what he learned in this
way lingered in his memory, testimony to the utility of an
earlier era's family diversions—activities that demanded
children *participate,* working their imaginations—even,
perhaps, thinking. Great-Aunt Eliza Stuart might cultivate Marshall's attention with small bribes for learning
catechism, but her labors, and those of the two private
tutors who succeeded her, "so soured me on study and
teaching that I like never to have recovered from them,"
Marshall once remarked.[5]

Marshall, who was to later earn a reputation as perhaps the best and most devoted teacher in the army, can
be forgiven for a mildly disingenuous explanation of his
scholastic abilities. It is reasonable to infer that hearing
Cooper and Scott read aloud was infinitely more useful
to the adult soldier than the unhappy labors demanded
of him by schoolmasters. By such means did Marshall
and his generation learn and cultivate a taste for reading history and biography that nourished their imaginations and informed their judgments over a lifetime: the

generation that embraced wartime colleagues like Lord
Alanbrooke, Winston Churchill, John Dill, George Patton, and Eisenhower.

One cannot help but recognize, even at first glance,
the stark difference between this generation's means of
formation and those of more recent times. In these differences do we find the clues to many of our contemporary ills, few of which compare in detriment to the
nation's character than an unmistakable lack of appreciation for, or outright hostility to, learning from the great,
if imperfect, figures and works of the past.

At seven years of age, Marshall was taken to meet
the superintendent of local schools to determine his fitness and placement in an appropriate class. The superintendent posed rudimentary questions in English and
mathematics. Marshall was unable to answer any of
them. His father was mortified. Marshall, as he readily admitted, did not like school. Worse, he sensed the
paternal humiliation caused by the distance between his
scholastic abilities and the unspoken academic success
of his older brother. Over the next few years, George Jr.
would earn and sustain an honest reputation for being a
mediocre student at best.

.   .   .

In 1890 George Marshall Sr. and his business partners,
looking for working capital for new projects, decided

to sell certain holdings to Henry Clay Frick, by now a coal magnate of fabulous wealth. Frick demanded that the partners throw in one of their subsidiary businesses, formed in 1888, the Kyle Coke Company. The partners realized a large profit from the sale, of which Marshall's share was $150,000, a huge sum for those days. Immediately (and ignoring Laura Marshall's counsel) he committed almost all this windfall to a mid–Shenandoah Valley land and realty venture near Luray, Virginia. A large tract would be subdivided and sold for vacation properties near the famous Luray Caverns; the lots would be advertised in cities of the mid-Atlantic and northeastern states.

The venture failed almost immediately. In the volatile economy of the late-nineteenth century, demand had simply collapsed. The company folded—indeed its showplace, the Luray Inn, a kind of Greenbrier or Homestead for its time, burned down. Marshall lost nearly all his money, not excluding personal loans he had taken out to help shore up the company's finances. Of all his substance, he was barely able to salvage enough to sustain the family. George Jr. recalled: "We had to economize very bitterly."[6] At an age when children are notoriously sensitive to such things, the Marshall family had to make severe changes in the way they lived.

Surely a consequence of George Marshall Jr.'s lifelong solicitude for his own family finances was his refusal to even countenance the appearance of some idle luxury or indulgence. All his life he would keep detailed accounts of allocations from his monthly army salary. He would remain particularly sensitive to the financial burden—often amounting to outright penury—borne by enlisted men in the lowest grades. In 1947, as secretary of state, finding that the State Department had rented him a suite at the Waldorf Astoria, he insisted on being moved at once to the far less grand Hotel Pennsylvania near Grand Central Terminal. In late 1945, on a visit of reunion with his second wife, Katherine Marshall, to the Frenchwoman who had looked after him and several other young officers on John Pershing's staff twenty-five years earlier, he refused to allow his wife to make a gift for Madame Jouette of her fur coat—as chief of staff of the United States Army, he had not made enough to put anything by; the Marshalls had had to dip into their earlier savings to underwrite social obligations.

.   .   .

In early adolescence Marshall began to withdraw, in well-disguised ways, from the easy traffic of social inter-course. His circle of friends contracted. Always per-ceived as shy and bashful, and his difficulties in school well-known, he began to cultivate a certain solitude of spirit, a reserve, that would become a settled part of his adult character. This was not so much the solitude of removal from company but the deliberate withholding of self and a quiet determination to strike out on his own, to define some path, to acquire some unusual expertise, to remove himself from the interests and knowledge of adults around him. Neither ignorable vocation nor unsought epiphany decided him on a military career: "career" had no meaning to him in any case. The process, if it may be so called, was longer and more diffuse and, as with most peacetime adolescent intentions to join "the military," had little basis in Marshall's knowledge of the regular army or with what it was that soldiers of his day actually *did*. In this regard, Marshall's exact contemporary, Douglas MacArthur, who had literally been born into the army, knew exactly what he wanted, and what it meant. The things that led Marshall not only did not imply a lifelong commitment but also had relatively little to do with the army.

The major predisposing factor to his joining the army was a determination to distinguish himself in some field for which he sensed his character and talents—which did not include academic aptness—would suit him, and in which he could prove himself. It is an ageless family phenomenon: "I'll show them." For Marshall, the "them" was his older brother and father, both of whom doubted his aptitude for business or for any other profession for which the intellectual acuity that declares itself by verbal facility seems prerequisite. But tenacity, will, resolution ("You may be whatever you resolve to be," in Stonewall Jackson's formulation), once mobilized on behalf of ambition, could make such ambition formidable. The father, unenthusiastic about George's declared bent, acquiesced nonetheless. Cultivation of the martial virtues seemed somehow to attract his son, as their cultivation had appealed to earlier generations of Marshalls: self-denial, hardihood, courage, absorption in some great cause. Here the allure of the Marshall heritage must have been persuasive. It would be a road not taken for two generations of Marshalls, but it was a road still sturdy and serviceable. It was a career to whose demands he might be suited, an enterprise in which he might gain an authority that would provide him a measure of control. He had been bruised repeatedly as a boy: not in traumatic ways, not as the consequence of a malicious paternal intent or deliberate acts of humiliation, but rather as the younger brother who had not quite measured up. Like another great soldier of an earlier generation—U. S. Grant, who died when Marshall was four—he had lived as a child at the observant edge of things, always quick and clever at withdrawing from social circumstances in which adults might ask questions.

In the simplest of chronologies, the young George Marshall was closer to the American Civil War than an American of the early twenty-first century is to Vietnam. He was nearer to Appomattox than a youth of 2017 is to the fall of Saigon. Uniontown, so close to what was once Virginia (after 1863, West Virginia), had furnished dozens of soldiers to the Union cause; many of them were now veterans still in their late forties. They were heroes, local icons, patriots whose service was celebrated annually in colorful parades and reunions. The Grand

Army of the Republic was the most powerful alumni association in the country. Famous generals, South and North, were still living: honored, outspoken, always visible. One Uniontown citizen, James Hustead, the father of one of Marshall's boyhood chums, had commanded a Union battery at the Battle of New Market, Virginia, in May 1864. From his position just across the North Fork of the Shenandoah he had watched the famous charge of the VMI cadets against the Union center, a charge then, and still, much celebrated in Southern history. "If I have a son," Hustead declared, "I will send him to that school." He did. George Jr., having himself walked over the old battlefield, heard his brother talk of the hardships of his cadetship and how he had overcome them.

Neither father nor son ever considered seriously George Jr.'s applying to United States Military Academy at West Point (USMA), the only regular source of new lieutenants for the tiny army of the mid-1890s. The father's Democratic affiliations and convictions were well-known; both senators and congressmen were Republicans. Nor could George Jr. have been expected to perform creditably on the entrance examinations used by congressmen to rank the candidates for each district. There was, further, the matter of a childhood injury, never properly healed, to Marshall's elbow: he might not have passed the physical. So VMI was not only an obvious choice, it was the only choice. And the superintendent, Brigadier General Scott Shipp, himself a wounded veteran of the New Market battle, was far less interested in academic credentials than in what he could learn, if he did not already know, about the character and antecedents of applicants. Like many headmasters and college leaders of the nineteenth century, he believed blood and heritage trumped cleverness and academic success, however hard-won.

In early September 1897, the Marshalls, Stuart and Marie included, drove George Marshall Jr. to the railroad station in Connellsville, a dozen miles from Uniontown. The boy—he was still sixteen—clambered up the steps to the passenger car on the Charlottesville train, turned and waved to his family, and disappeared. He bore a letter from his father to the superintendent, certainly the tenderest thing Mr. Marshall had ever confided about his son: "I send you my youngest and my last. He is bright, full of life, and will, I believe, get on quite well."[7]

Chapter Two

Marshall at VMI

I have always thought that one Man of tolerable
Abilities may work great changes, and accomplish
great Affairs of Mankind, if he first forms a good
plan, and, cutting off all Amusements and other
Employments that would divert his Attention, makes
the Execution of that same Plan his sole Study and
Business.

—Benjamin Franklin, *Autobiography*[1]

Retained as an expert witness during the 1990s legal
battle between VMI and the Department of Justice over the admission of women cadets, the sociologist
David Riesman argued that colleges that most decisively
intervene in the lives of their students are those of an
unusual, distinctive culture and ethos: singular places
with long-serving teachers (many of whom are "characters"), cherished and ancient eccentricities, and adamant

allegiance to the work of forming "character" as well as educating the mind. VMI qualified as such a singular place; that singularity should not, he argued, be put at risk. Riesman's arguments were insufficiently persuasive. The Supreme Court ruled, by a vote of 7–1, that no applicant could be denied admission on the basis of gender. Its decision was implemented exactly a hundred years after the matriculation of George Catlett Marshall Jr. as a new cadet. He entered a school that had changed very little since its founding on the site of an old arsenal in 1839: woman cadets apart, he would have discovered, thirty-eight years after his death in 1959, a school changed very little since he matriculated in 1897.

He arrived at VMI on September 11, 1897. It was late afternoon, a windless humid day. He was alone. His 122 classmates, "brother rats," had matriculated a week earlier. Marshall's late arrival, excused by the authorities, had allowed time for a not quite full recovery from a case of typhoid fever.

Upon arrival, there can be no doubt that Marshall paused at the Limits Gates marking the western boundary of the institute. Before him lay a prospect of majestic austerity. Two hundred yards away, at the far boundary of the great parade ground, stood the VMI barracks, its facade a glowing creamy ocher, the building dominated by towers, octagonal turrets, at the corners, each crenellated like the walls of a medieval fortress. The west front of the barracks was defined by oblong mullioned windows marking each cadet room and was, and remains, the most recognizable feature of the post. It commanded the parade ground and communicated both the romance of the school's history and a severe purposiveness: glory and severity—each indispensable to the other. The parade ground, large enough to accommodate a small army, would have been fragrant with rich late-summer smells, and Marshall would surely have been conscious of the huge eminences behind and to his left—the shouldering hills of the Alleghenies, dusty and purple in the afternoon haze.

The barracks lay near the house of the superintendent and commandant, both built in the same neo-Gothic idiom as the rats' temporary homes. And, framed by all three, the evolutions of marching cadets now proclaimed some sort of review or guard mounting in progress, the cadets responding to the adjutant's commands, marching in that limber athletic gate so distinctly American: marching in perfect but easy step, their movements without European stiffness. They were resplendent in dress gray coatees with white cross-dykes (belts that lay diagonally across the chest), white trousers, plumed shakos, and rifles.

Perhaps Marshall remembered that the barracks had been rebuilt, and recently. It had been bombarded and almost destroyed on the orders of the Union general David Hunter in the summer of 1864, for whom the institute was, it was said, "a nest of vipers—where the worst of the Rebels come from." An artillery captain, Henry A. DuPont, had remonstrated with Hunter, arguing against the bombardment. Seventeen years later, as Senator DuPont, of Delaware, he secured restitution from Congress. The funds were used to restore the building.

The VMI of 1897 was a brutal place. Living conditions were beyond austere. The interior of the barracks, configured like a kind of prison, reminded a visitor of Jeremy Bentham's panopticon, a prison in which all inmates could be watched at all times by hidden monitors. Outdoor galleries overlooked a courtyard. Each gallery, or stoop, was assigned lodging for each class: seniors, first classmen, on the ground floor; rats, fourth classmen, on the fourth floor. The rats, therefore, were exposed to the abuse and hazing of all three upper classes as they drove the steps to meet formations and respond to the calls of nature or the demands of upperclassmen. Marshall's situation was worse: his class, unusually large for the day, overflowed onto the third stoop. This meant a constant exposure to the taunts, demands, and abuse of young men who had just finished their own rat trials. This was a sort of military baptism by fire.

This Marshall could hardly be called a man. Only sixteen, he was soon marked out for special attention. Stuart had graduated three years earlier—few remembered him, but Marshall's Pittsburgh twang, his speech distinguished by flattened, bitten-off vowels, marked him as a Yankee, his name notwithstanding. The superintendent, General Shipp, "Old Billy," wrote in a note to Mr. Marshall that he had seen the son soon after his arrival, and that "he already looks like a soldier." This, it should be said, is very dubious. Marshall looked like any rat: awkward, pale, skinny, and scared.

Early in his first term, Marshall was tested in a hazing ritual then common to West Point and VMI: a small group of upperclassmen, in a barracks room, forced him to squat over a bayonet—its handle braced on the floor and the tip just touching Marshall's buttocks. The idea was to make a new cadet maintain this position as long as possible, with upperclassmen intervening to stop the activity when they judged the rat was about to collapse. Maintaining such a position is especially hard for a long-legged cadet (Marshall was about five feet eleven inches), and almost impossible for a cadet in his weakened condition. The inevitable happened. The bayonet penetrated one side of Marshall's buttocks. He bled profusely and was rushed to the school dispensary. In what became the earliest chapter of the Marshall legend, however, the new cadet refused to oblige a doctor who asked how such a terrible wound had been incurred. Marshall would not give names. Thereafter, his exposure to serious hazing was abruptly reduced.

. . .

Near the end of his life George Marshall was asked whether his not having gone to West Point had blighted

his early career in the army. No, he said, because VMI
had always been considered rather "distingué" by West
Pointers: they thought it was a singular place, fiercely
military, "the West Point of the South," linked in many
ways to the academy. A VMI graduate who gained a
commission was assumed to be serious about soldiering.
In 1903, in the tiny officer corps of the day, there were
only twenty-seven VMI men on active duty. These men
were nevertheless known as able and industrious, and
their success was out of proportion to their numbers.

The institute's mission differed radically from West
Point's. Its purpose was to use military training to achieve
civilian ends: to use such training as a means of inculcat-
ing elements of self-command, the virtue that would find
its usefulness in civil life.[2] At the same time, graduates
would be ready, "in every time of the deepest peril," to
serve as citizen officers. Like Cincinnatus, an institute
hero, they would then return home, unheralded and with
the sense that they had done nothing other than their
duty. It was a stern ethos, and one that pervaded the
institute's culture.

But while the missions of VMI and West Point were
different, the similarities were striking. VMI's founders
included West Point men, and its first superintendent,
Francis H. Smith, was a graduate, USMA class of 1833.
He became one of those craggy Victorian headmasters
and presidents distinguished by very long tenures (fifty
years at VMI), indefatigable energy, remorseless devotion to duty, uprightness of character—and granitic ded-

ication to the institute's mission: "He who has obtained a mastery of himself to discharge the smallest duty has done much to qualify himself for the greatest," Smith once said. The preparation and strengthening of character, Smith believed, was an obligation of education at least as important as the training and cultivation of mind. Smith visited Europe and England before taking up his duties, studying European methods, buying books and apparatus, and visiting, among other places, Dr. Thomas Arnold's Rugby School, whose mission must have struck him as directly pertinent to his own purposes for VMI. To say that VMI's leaders were central to sustaining its mission would be no exaggeration; Smith is one of many demonstrative cases.

Through West Point there was also a strong early link with France, with L'École Polytechnique, one of whose graduates, Claudius Crozet, a Napoleonic officer, had taught engineering at the academy. He became a founding member of the VMI Board of Visitors, along with another zealous partisan of such forms of education—a lawyer from Lexington, Virginia, Colonel J. T. L. Preston. The VMI curriculum, like the academy's, would rely in its formation on the French allegiance to engineering, mathematical, and scientific subjects: practical training for practical men. For better or worse, there was no idle immersion in ancient languages and belles lettres.

VMI grew and flourished. Smith proved a tireless solicitor of funds from the commonwealth, and during VMI's most severe testing, 1861 to 1865, its graduates were prominent in dozens of actions small and large: some two thousand served in the Confederate armies, and a few fought for the Union. In the Army of Northern Virginia, they dominated the field-grade ranks. Stonewall Jackson, a VMI faculty member from 1851 to 1861, was amazed at the number of VMI men in the field with him at Chancellorsville (where he received his mortal wound on May 10, 1863). Some thirteen (of fifteen) regimental commanders in George Pickett's doomed division at Gettysburg were VMI men. Most deeply cherished in the institutional memory, however, was the cadet battalion's service at New Market, Virginia (May 15, 1864), the only major action ever fought by an American school or college. At New Market, 247 cadets, many Marshall's age or even younger, marched some eighty miles down the Shenandoah Valley to join a scratch army of about five thousand Confederates under General John C. Breckinridge, whose mission was to block a Union force under General Franz Sigel heading south with orders to capture the town of Staunton and cut rail communications to the east.

"Put the boys in," ordered Breckinridge, "and God forgive me for the order." Ten cadets were killed in the battle, forty-seven wounded—most in a charge from the Confederate center that overran a Union battery and was credited with helping to turn the tide of the battle. Cadets of Marshall's generation often saw and knew veterans of this and other Confederate campaigns and battles; some were men who served on the VMI faculty. George Marshall, that is to say, knew and heard of officers who had served with Robert E. Lee and Stonewall Jackson—both of whom were buried in the town of Lexington.

Like his exact contemporary, Douglas MacArthur (born in 1880, USMA class of 1903), and like Robert E. Lee (USMA class of 1829), Cadet Marshall would go through four cadet years without a demerit. Such prodigies of perfect adherence to regulations are a bit less impressive than they seem. Avoiding the big penalties would have been no trick for such men—self-disciplined, model cadets who, when and if they did test the limits, knew how to minimize risk. But keeping clear of demerits given for small deviations from standards was much more difficult. These were commonly assigned for "room deficiencies" (cadet rooms were inspected daily). "Skins," or "bones," were awarded for tiny deficiencies, some of them absurd. Books not arranged in descending order of height. Dust on the rifle rack. Dirty bore (the rifle, not the cadet). The list could continue.

Here George Marshall was blessed with sympathetic roommates all four years at VMI. They understood from the start that he was determined to excel as a cadet. A deal was arranged, common then and still: "military" cadets often room with classmates not given to punctilios of perfect order; Marshall (or MacArthur) arranged for the less "military" roommates to sign on as permanent room orderlies; all demerits are awarded the latter. Marshall, as his side of the bargain, offered tutoring or some other benefit in return.

.   .   .

The academic curriculum of the institute was not terribly demanding. Again, it reflected the school's indebtedness to the military academy, and its proud sense of itself as an engineering college. The Marshall of mature years would, like Churchill, indulge the idle fiction of his schoolboy inaptness for academic labors: "Frankly, I didn't like any subject best. In trying to think about it, I can't recall one that pleased me."[3] But this is not quite true. Marshall liked English and history (taught together as a single course during his third-class year). He may not have "liked" French, and his efforts at communicating in the language during service in France were so comically inept that he resolved never to use the language again, but, at VMI, he stood eighth out of fifty-six in French. Further, Marshall appears to have had slender aptitude for engineering, mechanics, physics, and chemistry. He would graduate a respectable fifteenth of the thirty-three classmates who completed the four-year academic curriculum, and fifth among the eighteen graduates in civil engineering.

Military school academic successes cast meager illumination on talent and potential. Proficiency in things

like fluid mechanics would seem to have the same usefulness in an infantry officer as organic chemistry might
provide a broker on the floor of the stock exchange: none.
But Marshall indulged an avid interest in history at the
institute, and here, as in other circumstances, he was fortunate in his assigned roommates: Leonard K. Nicholson,
whose family owned the New Orleans *Times-Picayune,*
and, the following year, Philip B. Peyton—"Buster"—a
future general officer, but, in cadet days, fun-loving and
slack in his military usages. Discarded review copies were
regularly sent to Nicholson by one of the newspaper's
editors, and the roommates read what they wished before
donating the books to the library. In later life, Marshall's
interest in history and his conviction that it was the most
important of academic and intellectual studies led him
to make impromptu talks on it. Occasionally, in fact, he
engaged Winston Churchill on historical topics when he
wanted to keep Churchill from talking about something
else. "What can you tell me about Warren Hastings?" he
would ask. This would distract Churchill for hours.

Marshall did excel, of course, in his assigned military subjects: military science and the art of war, US
drill regulations, among others. He shone in his military
duties as a cadet. Almost from the beginning he was a
marked man, stamped with a determination and earnestness that brother rats and upperclassmen respected.
During his days at VMI and all through his early years
as an army officer, Marshall exhibited a natural facil-

ity for pursuing military excellence—but in such a way as to excite admiration rather than envy or aggrieved competitiveness. Moreover, he undertook activities for which he had unexceptional gifts—notably football. He played on the varsity team as a guard, at 140 pounds, and earned accolades in the local papers for his spirited play against rivals like Virginia Tech and Washington and Lee. Marshall was a man of few athletic talents, but his determination nonetheless suited the profile of the young man: ambitious and driven, when he wanted to be.

Attrition at VMI was severe. Only 28 percent of Marshall's classmates survived the four-year course. Relatively few of those who left were brought low by academic failure. Then as now, many left offering tired rationales familiar to all generations of VMI administrators: "It's not for me," and, disingenuously, "I don't need this." Attrition reflected two things: a number of cadets had been put there by their families, and many were miserable. Hazing was continuous, trivial harassment constant, conditions of living Spartan, "minute regulation of behavior" (an avowed element of the school's educational ethos) unappealing. Summer furlough apart, there were no leaves and only four holidays a year. Cadets might visit Lexington on Saturday afternoon, but little divertissement was to be had in town—tidy and stern, a graceful artifact of the Scots-Irish migration up the valley from Pennsylvania more than a century earlier. Indeed, an alumnus of VMI described Lexington as he remembered it from his cadet days thirty-five years before Marshall's:

> The blue limestone streets looked hard. The red brick houses with severe stone trimming and plain white pillars ... were stiff and formal. The grim portals of the Presbyterian Church looked cold as a dog's nose. The cedar hedges ... [were] trimmed hard and close.... Furnished with an oaken hat-rack and straight oak chair of Gothic features.... On the walls are solemn engravings of Oliver Cromwell, Stonewall Jackson....[4]

The majority of Marshall's brother rats, and members of the classes just below his, were cadet privates. The cadet rank is an honorable station of the institute: a badge of independence, not a mark of military failure. These young men were not going to become army officers. In exercising his responsibilities, Marshall could not order them about like automatons. Getting them to do what was required or needed was excellent conditioning for future service in the army of a great democracy, one in which militarism and its sacramental fluorescences strike citizens as strange or alien, not admirable. The Marshall whom later generations would recognize and extol as an embodiment of a senior soldier for a democratic army, an army of civilians wearing uniforms for wartime service, learned how to lead such men—and, much later, women—at VMI. Those who today know anecdotally of Marshall, or even those who have read other biographies of him, will likely not appreciate his subsequent successes without knowing of his formative time at the institute, a time that set the stage for his leadership of soldiers for (and of) democracy.

.　　.　　.

What was Marshall like? Contemporaries remember him as earnest, good-hearted, rigorous in the execution of his duties. He addressed all but intimates by their last names. He seemed already to have begun cultivating the "cool, distancing courtesy" colleagues would experience years later, a kind of buffering that discouraged intimacy. With only a few friends—Nicholson and Peyton, for example—did the barrier come down. Marshall was investing his calling with exalted purpose: with a purpose and an ethic that must offer its satisfactions and sustain him through times of disillusionment and hardship. Few others lived or were drawn to such purpose. Marshall was becoming an artifact of his own conscious manufacture. Like such men as John Henry Newman and George Washington, he had decided at an early age: *This is the way I am going to be.* His reserve, his air of cautious reticence, created an aura much less of palpable militarism—bearing, "affect," abrupt assertiveness, et cetera—than of steady dutifulness. He was a *vir bonus:* upright, honorable, frank, calm, quiet. Duty, as Marshall conceived it, trumped all other temptations and needs, except one. Of successful generalship in a later war, the writer Correlli Barnett wrote that "only neutral factors of calculation" could be permitted to influence decisions. Marshall was well on his way to the embrace of such a credo. Much later, on becoming secretary of state in January 1947, he confided to his deputy, Dean Acheson, that his feelings were never to be spared. "I have no feelings except those I reserve for Mrs. Marshall," he once remarked.[5] (Mrs. Marshall was always referred to this way in George Marshall's letters.)

But this avowal, reverently recorded, is not quite true either: it was not true at VMI, nor during a long army career, or later. Marshall was never the figure of sober unemotionalism that pictures and accounts communicate. His friendships were intense, his empathies potent and unignorably so, his loyalties profound. Their expressions most frequently took the form of tender letters bearing unexpected salutations or farewells, of elaborate personal courtesies, of favors, of friendships with children, of an overwhelming concern for ordinary soldiers. A week after Marshall's death, in October 1959, newspapers ran a Bill Mauldin cartoon illustrating especially clearly this latter dimension of Marshall's character: a Garand rifle is stuck upright before a battlefield grave, anchored by its bayonet. Willie and Joe—representatives of the American infantry that defeated Hitler—stand in sadness before a helmet stuck on the rifle's stock. On the helmet is the word MARSHALL.

Brother rats could hardly have failed to register another humanizing element in Marshall's last year at VMI. He was in love, so smitten that he began to run the block—to sneak out of barracks after taps—almost every night. This was a breach of regulations that, if discovered, would have reduced him to the rank of cadet private, destroyed his chances for commissioning, and, possibly, resulted in his dismissal from VMI. He had heard Elizabeth "Lily" Carter Coles playing the piano one soft evening as he walked back to barracks from a visit to town; the music reminded him of his mother's playing. Lily's house was at the edge of the post—here she lived with her mother, the widowed daughter of one of VMI's first graduates, Colonel Edmund Pendleton, who later became president of the institute's Board of Visitors.

They fell deeply in love and were married six months after Marshall's graduation from VMI.

Lily was several years older than George Marshall (she had once dated Stuart Marshall). She was something of an invalid. She had a thyroid condition linked, in the vague medical language and character of the day, to a heart condition. Strenuous activity was forbidden. It was understood that, at Lexington dances, "May I have this dance?" meant "May I sit with you, Lily?" She was the reigning belle of the town, beautiful and tall, remembered as witty and with an infectious sense of humor and little tolerance for the solemn and pompous. She and her mother had lived in Lexington ever since Lily's father suddenly died in St. Louis. Gay and effervescent in company, she was tender, almost motherly, with Marshall. Theirs would be a strong, terribly private, marriage. Notwithstanding, a contemporary heard her instruct First Captain George Catlett Marshall to "shut up, and let someone else talk." It is amazing to contemplate the solemn cadet leader being thus admonished: in the time of his later eminence, only Franklin Roosevelt, among colleagues in public life, ever called him "George." And even the president had tried it only once.

He had an extraordinary career at the institute—a cadetship, like Lee's and MacArthur's at West Point, that promised a military career of rare distinction. This was, however, provided that his time of service would furnish the wartime challenges needed to evoke and demonstrate qualities of mind and character equal, in positions of great responsibility, to their resolution. Marshall's undergraduate attainments were the consequence far less of academic aptitude than of qualities subsumed under "character": tenacity of purpose, integrity, self-command, cultivated powers of concentration. He would finish as the outstanding man of the class of 1901, and recognized as such (though without academic accolade). These virtues were the product, at least in part, of Marshall's formative years at the institute—ones that had been introduced in the boy's youth and developed through the rigors of his education.

Marshall graduated on June 26, 1901, in Jackson Memorial Hall. He received his diploma from General Shipp, and heard—typical for the time—a passionate eulogium to Stonewall Jackson by a local judge: "When the great captain died, thousands wept over the grave where genius and goodness and valor slept with him ... and when the time comes that another Jackson is demanded, the Institute will furnish him."[6]

.   .   .

VMI might be the West Point of the South, but graduation from the institute did not lead reliably or easily to an army commission. Cadets of Marshall's generation were, however, favored by timing. The Spanish-American War, fought and won in 1898, was followed by a prolonged, deadly insurrection in the Philippines, which had been ceded by Spain to the United States at the end of the war. The consequence was a series of decisions in Congress, guided by Elihu Root, the new secretary of war, that would, among other important reforms, increase the size of the permanent regular army establishment. This, in turn, required the recruitment of several hundred new lieutenants. West Pointers and volunteer officers from the late war would have priority in the selection procedures; the remaining "slots" would be filled by those selected, by competitive examination, from among men without prior service. One hundred forty-two vacancies remained in the spring of 1901, and Marshall mobilized his resources to secure a commission to fill one of the openings.

The candidates themselves had to be selected by competitive process established by each state, and their names forwarded for authorization to take the tests. To protect himself, Marshall—who would not turn twenty-one until the end of 1901 and could not therefore be commissioned until the turn of the year—now had recourse to that familiar refuge of the unemployed gentleman graduate: teaching in a preparatory school, in this instance at the Danville Military Institute (a small school for boys). He was awarded the rank of major, made commandant of cadets, and assigned to teach a variety of subjects. This is ironic, in one sense, given the educational challenges of his youth.

The elder Marshall, as ever labile in his judgments of his youngest son's ambitions and prospects, now flung himself heart and soul into the complicated enterprise of securing a commission for the younger. He arranged for Marshall to visit Pennsylvania's highly placed in government in Washington. He wrote the commonwealth's senators. For his part, his son, during his Washington visitation, contrived to attach himself to a party of visitors to President William McKinley's office in the White House. When the group left, he stayed behind to plead his case. John Wise—son of the governor of Virginia, New Market cadet, and now prominent lawyer in New York—wrote on Marshall's behalf to the department commander in New York, a major general in charge of administering the examinations, urging Marshall's suitability for commissioning. "General Shipp regards him as one of the fittest pieces of food for gunpowder turned out by his mill for many years," he wrote.[7]

The exams were not hard. They comprised mathematics, history, English literature, and grammar. Rather larger weight was given to "physique" and "moral character and antecedents." Marshall attained a net score of 84.8, one of the highest results. Another letter from Wise prompted the army to notify Marshall of his good fortune, informing him that he would be commissioned early in 1902 (backdated to February 2, 1901—the date of the enabling act of Congress). Requesting a commission in the prestigious artillery branch, Marshall was notified that he would be an infantry officer, that he was to join the Thirtieth Infantry Regiment, now in the Philippines, and that he was to report for duty at Fort Myer, Virginia, thence to begin his long journey to the Far East.

He was now free to marry. The wedding in Lexington was celebrated at Lily's home, from which the couple, standing on the porch, could see the VMI barracks. The whole Marshall entourage had come down from Pennsylvania, not excluding Stuart, to witness the ceremony. Four years earlier they had driven the youngest sibling to the train station to begin his military career. They now witnessed the happiest elements of its fulfillment: commissioning, marriage, and the assignment that Marshall, however much in love he may have been, surely craved—duty with troops, overseas, in the zone of war.

Chapter Three

Early Service, Philippines

Whig history, not seriously practiced after Auschwitz, posits a world in a continuing state of improvement. Each generation takes satisfaction in seeing how far it has come, and in how ably it has employed the lessons offered by those preceding. It is difficult not to yield to a collateral temptation in studying the later careers of Marshall and his contemporaries in the army with respect to how they employed lessons they learned in the two world wars. Like most regulars commissioned around the turn of the twentieth century, however, Marshall would be a lieutenant for many years before the wars. His first tour of duty was ten thousand miles from the Shenandoah Valley: the Philippines.

From May 1902 to November 1903, Marshall was provided with a crowded plenitude of experiences and challenges in cultures utterly strange to him: that of the islands themselves, and that of long-service, hard-bitten American regular soldiery. Like a freshly graduated Victorian schoolboy, he had been sent out to answer the needs of a new American empire, but much of that answering would have neither the benefit of experienced advice nor the assurance of firm support from superiors. For much of his time in the Philippines, Marshall *had* no superior. The nearest senior officer was in Manila. Marshall was weeks away.

President Theodore Roosevelt had proclaimed the islands pacified on July 4, 1902. The insurrection that had followed America's war with Spain in the Philippines was, officially at least, over. A majority of American volunteer regiments had long since gone home, and the remainder of the army's regulars—Marshall's Thirtieth Infantry soldiers among them—now numbered only forty thousand men. These were distributed in some five hundred outposts among the numberless islands of the archipelago, typically in places so remote that their only communications with Manila, generally with their own commanders, were by sea. Marshall noted an effective turnaround of about two months (that is, the time from his dispatch of a report or request until the arrival of an effective response). The climate was enervating, rations meager and unvarying, sickness pervasive (cholera, malaria, and dengue fever were common, as was a rich variety of unpleasant skin ailments), the routine negating and stifling. Privates were paid $13 a month; new lieutenants $116. Combats with an elusive and not wholly pacified enemy were sporadic, and almost always instigated by small bands of outlaws, or ladrones. Assured he need not worry about such dangers, Lieutenant Douglas MacArthur was ambushed on a Leyte patrol immediately after his arrival for duty. Two Visayan guerrillas fired at him from point-blank range, missing his head by less than an inch; he then shot them both dead. His experience was common, though his recollection of the early days in the Philippines was not. He remembered how he cherished "the languorous laze that seemed to glamorize even the most routine chores of life, and fun-loving men, the moonbeam delicacy of its lovely women, [which] fastened me with a grip that has never relaxed."[1]

The war and the Philippine Insurrection (1899–1902) offered Marshall's generation the first experience of active service. These conflicts stood in the same chronological relationship to Marshall's cohort (which included Douglas MacArthur, Joseph Stilwell, Jonathan Wainwright, and Walter Krueger) that the Mexican War (1846–1848) bore to that of Ulysses S. Grant, William Tecumseh Sherman, Stonewall Jackson, and James Longstreet. By their late twenties, young officers of both generations had gained valuable experience and had begun forming relationships with contemporaries and superiors who would, many years hence, serve them usefully in subsequent conflicts. Much of the latter generation's experience was earned in circumstances of isolation: crucibles, we might say, of character.

Despite the evident chronological parallels, there were significant differences between Grant's and Marshall's generations. One was the country's full-throated exuberance in its opportunity to fight Spain, and in the attendant service, morally satisfying to Americans of the time, of cleansing and saving Cuba from its cruel overlords. Grant's generation had no such illusion about its war. It fought courageously and successfully, but it was skeptical of the justification for such a war.

Marshall's generation was troubled not at all. The Hearst press had clamored for war, particularly after the explosion that sank the battleship *Maine* in Havana Harbor—an explosion, it was said, caused by a Spanish mine. By the end of April 1898, ten weeks after the *Maine* disaster, President McKinley, with a demure show of reluctance in requesting an appropriate response, had asked for and received congressional assent to the proposition that, since Spain had already broken diplomatic relations with the United States, a state of war had existed from that date. Thus McKinley could order George Dewey's Asiatic Fleet, now at Hong Kong, to destroy the Spanish fleet at its anchorage in Manila Bay: "You may fire when ready, Gridley." Five days later, the decrepit Spanish fleet lay at the bottom of the bay. America rejoiced, though the famous Mr. Dooley confessed most of his countrymen didn't "know whether the Philippines were islands or canned goods."[2]

The country expected the islands would be granted their independence. This was not the president's intention. An American infantry force under General Wesley Merritt forced a Spanish surrender on July 17, and by the Treaty of Paris on December 8, Spain was forced to cede the whole archipelago to the United States—in return for a sum of twenty million dollars.

The United States, historians frequently argue, had been enchanted by what John Quincy Adams once called "the murky radiance of dominion and power." It had now reignited a potent insurgency under Emilio Aguinaldo, who, with a force of revolutionaries at one time prepared to welcome American intervention, soon became its enemies. This insurgency would last until midsummer 1902, about the time Marshall arrived for duty. He had been touched by the war during his first year at VMI. The corps volunteered its services to the president and, a year later, he had been present for the return from Philippine duty of the Tenth Pennsylvania Infantry, considered a crack regiment. One of its companies, comprising many men from Uniontown and its environs, paraded through the town. Marshall was thrilled.

Marshall sailed from San Francisco on April 12, 1902, on the transport ship *Kilpatrick*. The trip out, long and languid, had by now become a regular ceremonial of transpacific service, a voyage of thirty-five to forty days, with occasional stops in Hawaii and Nagasaki. Passenger rosters contained a jumbled assemblage of older officers with wives and children and nannies, unaccompanied younger officers, bachelors, civilian professionals of one kind or another, noncommissioned officers (NCOs), and soldiers. Among them were veterans returning for second and even third tours of duty. Lieutenant Joe Stilwell remembered his ship being filled with "the booze fighters who got tanked every night ... one soaking like a piece of milk toast."[3] There was furtive shipboard romancing; bridge games, shuffleboard, amateur theatricals; and ample time for blowhards to instruct those going out for the first time. "They were very industrious in telling me," Marshall noted, "how I should function. They understood it all. Later on I discovered they knew damned little."[4]

.   .   .

Almost immediately, less than two days after arriving in Manila, virtually without funds, without tropical kit or specified assignment, Marshall received orders to report to Mindoro, a Connecticut-size island south of Luzon. Here, the Thirtieth Infantry had assigned several companies to search for dispersed members of the insurrection (Mindoro was a common destination for these fugitives), and to offer the local population some security from their depredations. The trip to the island began inauspiciously: in a five-day quarantine on a filthy, greasy interisland steamer in broiling heat. Once underway, a major typhoon almost sank the ship and obliged Marshall and another lieutenant to man the bridge, the captain having fled below in terror.

Safely landed, Marshall found himself in the rough community of Calapan, "capital" of the island and headquarters of one of the Thirtieth's battalions. There were several officers, including a new colonel in command, a veteran of the Civil War. Morale was awful. The post was quarantined, enemy action rare, the colonel's predecessor a hated martinet. As for the soldiers, Marshall later called them "the wildest crowd I've seen before or since." They were long-serving regulars, mostly privates, many who had done time in the stockade. The new colonel, Marshall, and a few others had the overwhelming responsibility of saving this crowd from the consequences of a deadly, widespread cholera epidemic now sweeping the Philippines. This epidemic would cause many thousands of deaths before running its course. Evidences of its work were everywhere: fresh graves, coffins piled up, overflowing hospitals, onerous restrictions on movement, rigid requirements for boiling everything. Cholera's causes were as baffling to contemporaries as its cure was unknown. The onset of the disease was sudden and overwhelming: men sickened at dusk and were discovered dead at reveille. The equivalent of a leper colony was set up two miles from the village to separate the sick from the healthy. Dr. Fletcher Gardner, with whom Marshall shared a billet, informed Marshall one night that he himself expected to be dead in the morning; he had felt the onset of symptoms, but it was a false alarm. Through stringent management of the quarantine, the Calapan garrison came through with but one death.

Like Ensign Pulver in *Mister Roberts,* Marshall was now handed a mission typically used to test a second lieutenant's mettle: he was to organize a field day and accompanying entertainments for the dispirited soldiers of the garrison, part of a ginned-up celebration of July Fourth and the end of the quarantine. The assignment was fortuitous. From the start of his army career, Marshall was to exhibit an earnest and hearty liking for such things—field days, amateur theatricals, fox hunts, treasure rides, family outings. He had the naïf's earnestness and goodwill, things that immunized him against ridicule and envy, and he had brought with him the confidence of the recently graduated cadet officer. With a large purse of money to which the senior NCOs and officers had contributed, Marshall sought competitors for a hundred-yard dash. The sullen NCOs and privates held back and only two men entered. Marshall split the whole purse between the victor and the runner-up; thereafter participation became robust, and Marshall persuaded the new colonel that it would be perceived as an act of salutary kindness to release, from the local stockade, a soldier who had been allowed to entertain the garrison (he was a singer). This commended the colonel to the garrison, and the new lieutenant to his colonel.

About this time, Lieutenant Marshall led a small patrol to an island just off the southern Mindoro coast, responding to a sighting of a band of ladrones supposedly hiding out there. En route the patrol came upon a native pony being stitched up after an attack by a crocodile. Soon after, in the middle of a stream crossing, one of the soldiers shouted "Crocodile!" The patrol, which had been wading across in a single file, panicked, trampling over Marshall as they clambered toward the far bank. Marshall's response, much admired when he reported back, was to fall the men in—in formation and at attention—and then march them back and forth across the stream. This was a simple but intelligent lesson in discipline. Incidents like these, magnified in the subsequent telling, were adduced as evidence that the young officer was resourceful, already confident in the exercise of authority (it may be assumed that most of the men were older than he), and therefore a reliable soldier who would bear watching.

The hard school of dutifulness offered continuous tuition. Until the late-twentieth century, young soldiers were terribly underpaid, and all through American history, they have been used as common laborers when no other sources of labor have been available. Marshall, testifying before a congressional committee about an appropriations bill between the world wars, remembered an incident from his Philippine service; he used it in making his case. During his assignment at Mangarin, a coastal village at the southern end of Mindoro where he was sent after Calapan, he was responsible for seeing that a requirement of the Quartermaster Department in Manila be obliged. The interisland steamer, a rusted hulk that visited the garrison every three or four weeks, had to take on coal. The crew's contract exempted them from manual labor ashore. The consequence was that the soldiers of the tiny garrison had to move the coal from its storage bins on the coast—first sacking it, then carrying it to a single, narrow flat-bottomed boat, loading the boat, and rowing it three-quarters of a mile to the steamer, then contriving means of getting it on deck—where the crew would handle it. Marshall told the committee what he remembered:

> One day while working in a torrential rain a tall, lanky soldier from the mountains of Kentucky paused in the middle of his shoveling job, with his comment: "I didn't see nothing like this on that damned recruiting circular." My old first sergeant suppressed a laugh, and flashed back the order to "Keep your mouth shut and shovel coal—that's your job." That gave me a lasting impression of the Regular Army, what discipline meant, what dependability meant in times of difficulty . . . there are times when the leader must command, "Keep your mouth shut and shovel coal; those are the orders."[5]

Marshall was always conscious of the difference between discipline (from the Latin root *discere,* "to learn") and obedience. The first sergeant demonstrated what discipline "meant," but for Marshall, such observations—lessons—came to imply something rather different. Forty-two years later, as chief of staff, he would hire Frank Capra to make army films in the series called *Why We Fight.* There is a plain connection between the scene on Mindoro in 1902 and the inspired decision in Washington, in 1943.

.   .   .

Halfway through his tour of duty in the Philippines, Marshall sent a letter to Scott Shipp. He had begun to sense in him both a proprietary interest in his career, and a prospective source of counsel, professional and also personal. He wrote him occasionally, sending him accounts of his work, impressions of the army, hints and, in one case, frank avowals of interest in returning to the institute as an assistant commandant. The letter to Shipp contains obligatory comments about his alma mater, but the important lines are these: "Mangarin was a very isolated post . . . but I found it agreeable from an official stand point, as I was left to my own judgment . . . I have found this life even pleasanter than I imagined it would be, and I think it will improve with time."

All his life, Marshall, functionally at ease among army colleagues and civilian superiors in government, would find solitude companionable. Like army contemporaries who would achieve high command in World War II, he would find in it something more: a school of self-reliance and the source of habituation to trusting his own judgment. Again, it was a life that conferred few material benefits if any; little in the way of generous praise, decoration, or—certainly—promotion. He was learning to make his own life.

.   .   .

Marshall was now ordered to join his assigned unit, Company G of the Thirtieth Infantry, then charged with the protection of Mangarin. "It was chiefly to safeguard the convent that a military post was set down in this otherwise isolated and desolate spot," Forrest Pogue wrote.[6] There was nothing there but a trailhead and a small convent run by the Recollect order, one sustained by a small farm. The company mission was "protection," but more than anything else, what needed to be protected and inspirited was the morale of a sulking, isolated garrison—of which Marshall was now in charge, the company commander having left, not to return to Mangarin for two months. Marshall became the sole authority on the southern half of the island, in effect its military governor. Acutely conscious of the distance he must maintain between himself and the enlisted men, without regular companionship, and with only routine garrison chores to supervise, Marshall and his NCOs were so remote from the world they had left behind that they forgot, until midafternoon, that December 25 meant Christmas.

Soon after his bleak Christmas in Mangarin, Marshall and the men he led were ordered to Manila, thence to a garrison near the city. He was given make-work assignments, some sufficiently menial to be remembered, years later, almost ruefully: "There isn't anything much lower than a second lieutenant and I was about the junior second lieutenant in the Army at that time."[7] He did, however, become a student of American military behavior abroad. In circumstances of occupation, much of what he saw appalled him—not only during his duties as an officer in charge of prisoners but also from stories that circulated about what Americans had done to enforce military rule on the islands. More often than not, these were terrible episodes in which, after taking fire from a town, the commander of a detachment ordered it burned to the ground. This is not even to mention the torching of a Catholic cathedral while American soldiers frolicked outside in the vestments of the priests: "Civilize 'em with a Krag." This was a long, long way from President McKinley's pious avowals of bringing the fruits of a beneficent democratic culture to America's new empire, or from Douglas MacArthur's women of moonbeam delicacy. In what had been an eighteen-month ceremony of lessons, perhaps none made a more lasting impression than these.

In mid-November 1903, the various elements of the Thirtieth Infantry were gathered in, brought to quarantine camps on Bataan, and loaded onto the transport *Sherman* for the long trip home via Nagasaki and Hawaii. After a reunion with Lily, in Virginia, Marshall reported to the real army in Fort Reno, Oklahoma Territory. This began yet another chapter in the formation of a leader.

Chapter Four

Fort Reno

From the clarifying perspective of another century, Marshall's early career comprises an orderly array of assignments and duties that together seem providential as means of preparation for the immense responsibilities that would follow forty years later. "He who has obtained the mastery over himself to meet and discharge the smallest duty, has done much to qualify himself for the greatest" was the bracing admonition of VMI's founding superintendent. The pronouncement perfectly suited a young officer of Marshall's character and ambition. He did not consciously undertake his duties in obedience to such strictures. Nor did he see his assignments as "early" or formative. They were duties to be carried out as capably as one could, and this implied an earnest determination to build a reputation for excellent performance in the things he was ordered to do. These assignments had a common character: they were to be executed in circumstances of isolation, they demanded self-reliance, they usually depended on Marshall's useful relationship with NCOs much older than himself, and they embodied responsibilities unusual for officers as young, as junior, as he.

The army to which Marshall returned, toward the end of December 1903, was scattered about more than fifty "posts," most in the Great Plains or in the Desert Southwest. Established in these places in the 1850s (and '60s, a few earlier), their original missions comprised the provision of escorts to westward migrant trains. Outstanding duties in the various territories and occasional "campaigns" against the Indians would also be required. By 1890, such requirements, however, had been dissipated: the noncitizens were either exterminated or settled on reservations, one of these in the Oklahoma Territory. This was Fort Reno.

At Fort Reno, Second Lieutenant Marshall was assigned to a remote garrison comprising several companies of infantry, now including his own, and a cavalry troop. The soldiers' mission was constabulary—they were to keep order by keeping an eye on the adjacent Indian reservation. Theirs was a world now lost to twenty-first-century America, its dying moments evoked in the paintings of Russell and Remington, the fiction of Owen Wister, and in regimental histories no longer read. Sixty years after Marshall's tenure at Reno, the post realized an ironic revitalization: as a prisoner of war camp for Wehrmacht veterans of the fighting in North Africa.

In 1903 Reno was one of the posts scattered about the

Great Plains and the Desert Southwest, all having out-lived their purposes, all subsisting in lives of unchalleng-ing routine: unchallenging to the most able. The frontier had been closed for fifteen years—around the time of the last great massacre of red men by white (at Wounded Knee, South Dakota). Comanche and Arapahoe fami-lies who lived on the reservation next to the post had long since settled into lives of desperate poverty, without prospects and sullenly acquiescent. Their army neigh-bors practiced the familiar military peacetime rigmarole of guard mountings, close-order drill, riflery, parades, and inspections: "the school of the soldiers." An ageless military obsession with order asserted itself: symmetries, tent-peg alignments, gleaming surfaces, immaculate uni-forms, polished stocks, curried mounts—outward signs, it was assumed, of a presumed interior grace and effi-ciency, of fitness for duty. But what duty? From time to time, company officers were given collateral duties—post engineer, ordnance officer, et cetera. Meantime, there was abundant leisure for the officers, for long rides along the Canadian River, for hunting; sometimes, after spells of rain, for fishing. Even Marshall recalled: "On one occa-sion when Mrs. Marshall and I were early for breakfast we heard quail calling in the sumac grove near us and I went out there and in about thirty minutes I had ten or twelve. . . ."[1]

Eighteen of these posts were served by three compa-nies of soldiers or fewer. These men, the younger among them now serving enlistments of three years, included large numbers of recent immigrants, mostly German or Scandinavian, all unmarried. Quarters and subsistence were provided to the enlisted men, neither much above a rough adequacy: grim wooden barracks, most as yet without electricity; iron bedsteads a foot apart; indifferent heating. The NCOs who were married occupied ramshackle cottages at the edge of the posts where their wives raised the children and took in the officers' laundry. A German observer, attached to an American regiment on maneuver in Texas, was struck by the absence of soldiers from the better classes. The American army's prestige, he reported, was very low indeed. Like earlier European visitors to the Great Republic—Alexis de Tocqueville and Anthony Trollope, for example—he also sensed the Americans' visceral antipathy to authoritarian discipline of the kind armies require. And for a country of seventy-five million, its size was tiny: 3,900 officers; 66,000 enlisted men.[2] Like Bismarck in the twentieth century, dismissing the British Army of Victorian times ("If they attacked, I'd have them arrested"), the visiting German could not imagine the American democracy's ever raising and training a potent military force.[3]

.   .   .

In the early summer of 1905, Marshall was sent from Fort Reno to Fort Clark, Texas, in response to an army requirement for the preparation of a progressive military map of the southwestern border, a vacant hinterland of supposed strategic consequence. He was to supervise the work of a team of several soldiers charged with the preparation of a map of two thousand square miles (larger than the state of Rhode Island). This was his team's contribution to a much grander effort.

The party entered a wilderness of blackened and rocky desert crosscut by deep ravines and studded with huge, bleak arroyos. The landscape was unwatered and treeless. Daytime temperatures touched 130 degrees. The methodology available was little advanced from that of Coronado and the conquistadores who had explored the same desert three hundred years earlier: "The time scale was the walking of my horse," wrote Marshall. A crude odometer was fashioned by measuring the circumference of a wagon wheel (for that part of the journey in which wagons could be used). At the beginning the party followed an unused railway; one of the soldiers was told to count ties. Fifty years later, Marshall would remember that it was the hardest service he would ever have in the army—and much of it was discharged on a diet of potatoes and onions, sometimes without water. When it was over, the party reported to the engineer captain at Fort Clark who had been charged with supervision of the map.

The captain at Fort Clark refused to believe Marshall was a commissioned officer. He had lost more than thirty pounds; his skin was burned to the color of rust; his uniform, bleached white, was in tatters; and a mule had eaten half his hat. An NCO vouched for him. The captain's superiors congratulated him on the thoroughness of his map—telling him it was the best of the submissions. Thirty-two years later, Brigadier General Marshall would report for duty as chief of war plans to the engineer captain: Malin Craig, now chief of staff of the army. A year and a half later, Marshall would succeed him.

.   .   .

Fort Reno's soldiers led lives, in the words of reforming Secretary of War Elihu Root, narrowing and dwarfing. It was Root whose bill for the expansion of the army in 1901, enacted in 1902, had made possible Marshall's appointment as second lieutenant. His achievements in creating a professional army with the novel mission of preparing itself for war, of rationalizing its structure of command and control—by the creation of a general staff and by providing for the continuing professional education of officers—rank him, with Henry Stimson and Newton Baker, as the most influential secretaries of war of the twentieth century. Stimson, Root's direct link to Marshall, would become Root's young law partner and, later, President Taft's secretary of war, from 1911 to 1913. It was an assignment Stimson undertook with pleasure, just as he accepted (thirty years later) the same commission from Franklin Roosevelt (1940).

Marshall had been a second classman (junior) at VMI in the summer of 1899—when, in July, Root took a phone call from the president. An aide, speaking on McKinley's behalf, inquired whether Root would gratify the president's wish that he take the position of secretary of war. Root responded that the president should be thanked for the request, but that the request was absurd because he knew nothing about war or the army.

After a pause, the aide responded for McKinley. The president was, in his telling, looking for a lawyer to direct the government of the Spanish island, rather than someone with expertise in warmaking or army management. Root acceded. He wrote to his friend Theodore Roosevelt, then governor of New York, that, despite having no desire for the role, he chose to answer the call to public service. He would hold the post for four and a half years.

Almost certainly by serendipity, McKinley had made an inspired choice in Elihu Root. He embodied a rare combination of qualities—temperament, character, a certain Benthamite case of mind—that sometimes makes for transformative administrative leadership of large, established organizations.

The army had defeated a sclerotic, third-rate power, Spain, and the country celebrated its easy victories in the Caribbean. On the whole, it believed itself fortunate in acquiring an empire in the Far East. But the winning of such easy victories had also uncovered appalling deficiencies in virtually every aspect of the army's leadership, organization, and performance. Hired to prescribe means by which the new territories could most efficiently be administered, Root now saw plainly that the means of administering the army were grossly inadequate for such labors. There was no agency responsible for planning or directing operations; logistical and armament resources were inadequate; there had been no comprehensive plan for transporting and training the 200,000 volunteers deployed. The relationship between the tiny regular army (28,000 officers and men in 1898) and the volunteers was unsatisfactory.

At his accession to the secretaryship, Root was fifty-four years old. He was the embodiment of a successful New York corporate lawyer, and a Republican. He was unself-advertising, knowledgeable, righteously austere, patriotic, blunt—"the brutal friend to whom I pay the most attention," Theodore Roosevelt once said.[4] His reputation for probity was matched by a reputation for industry and disinterestedness.

Though the president insisted that he wanted him in the position because Root (as a lawyer) could bring order to the administration of America's new overseas possessions, the new secretary soon discovered that the instrumentality by which the gains of the war were to be administered was largely to be, or rather depend upon, the regular army itself. This instrument, however, was not only unsuited to such a task, but it was also ill-suited to anything touching on what he, Root, assumed must be the work of an army: to prepare for and successfully prosecute the country's wars. During his long tenure under McKinley and Roosevelt, Root sought to impose principles of rationality on every aspect of the army that would serve that end: to prepare for and successfully prosecute war. He was assisted by a few sympathetic, reform-minded officers in Washington; these men were delighted by his appointment. Nevertheless, Root was opposed, as were his successors, by an odd assortment of outraged generals and colonels, many of them men who had been commissioned during the Civil War, who had grown comfortable and pompous in their billets. Many were far too old to execute their duties. They resisted Root's notions and reforms; some used their friendships with members of Congress to impede their implementation. Through an unusual combination of qualities of character (patience, tact, calm, tenacity of purpose), though, Root was able to effect many changes and to lay the groundwork for many others. In this work he was buoyed by the public's reaction to what it now realized had been a clouded, inglorious victory over Spain; a victory that had exposed the army's worst shortcomings.

Most troubling among the army's deficiencies was a culture, a system of command, that made useful cooperation among the various military authorities and agencies impossible. These were practices inherited from the infancy of the American Republic. The president was commander in chief, but only Congress could declare war. The president's principal military adviser, a member of his cabinet, was the secretary of war—charged with fiscal and administrative oversight of the army's activities. Such control was to be exercised through several staff bureaus in the capital: supply, ordnance, finance, pensions, et cetera. Another authority, in theory coequal with the secretary of war, was the commanding general. He, however, commanded nothing. Ordinarily the most famous general on the active list, he was charged with responsibility for the army's training and discipline and its command in wartime—which was nevertheless usually exercised in the field by other general officers. The commanding general had no authority over the bureaus (an exception was the adjutant general's office). He and the secretary of war were natural rivals. As one might expect, this was a recipe for an administrative nightmare, one certainly unbecoming of a nation whose imperial ambitions knew few limits.

No agency had responsibility for planning. No officer of a Washington bureau was obliged to return to field service after having been appointed to his new duties. As for the army "posts" themselves, no matter their small size or lack of suitability for their purposes, eliminating or consolidating them was next to impossible because of congressional insistence, state by state, that each be sustained. There was, finally, the question of manpower. The regular army was tiny. In theory, much larger forces might be drawn from the ranks of state militias in times of crisis, as they had been during the Civil War. But this system, its roots deep in the culture of colonial America and the Revolution, and in the national antipathy to standing armies, was completely unsuited to its prospective obligations. The war with Spain proved that.

These conditions were linked inextricably. The officers responsible were, by nature, reactionary. From time to time the strong and able had made the apparatus work—famously, the triumvirate of Lincoln, Grant, and Stanton. Later (in 1869), President Grant had, in fact, attempted to subordinate the bureaus to the commanding general—his friend Sherman—but his initiative was easily thwarted by Congress.

Root now set out to diagnose and to implement a prescription that would bring some sort of rationality to the whole. He began with the proposition, in his first annual report (1899), that the real object of having an army is to provide for war. To this novel observation he added the view that the regular army could never be expected to fight its country's wars without augmentation from the states, nor could it do so successfully without planning for contingencies.

.   .   .

During his term as secretary of war, Root initiated a series of reforms, ultimately forming and fashioning the structure of the American army whose chief of staff, forty years hence, would be George C. Marshall. What is most striking is the temperamental consanguinity of these two men: each would educate himself, in the bureaucratic language of a later day, "to work the system." Each had the disciplined patience to perform the acts of cultivation necessary to secure congressional approval for his prescriptions. Each assumed congressional superiors *not* to be adversaries but prospective allies. Each recruited generals to his cause: men admired in public service, brave and disinterested. Each allowed reactionary senior officers to make fools of themselves, but only once.

Root did not think of himself as a "progressive," though his diagnosis of the army's ills and his prescriptions for them placed him at the heart of the progressive movement. The fundamental purpose of an army is to prepare for war; all the "Root reforms" would flow from this purpose, diffusive in their effects, touching ultimately the very character of the American army itself. One does not often discuss *temperament* in accounting for the successes of reformers, but Root's, like his (later) law partner and successor as secretary of war, Henry Stimson's, would seem to have been ideal for his mission and program.

A settled antipathy toward change of any kind, not only "reform" but especially toward military learning and education, distinguished the culture of the senior officer corps after the war with Spain. Why, wondered the victors of Vicksburg, Mississippi, should the army change—in tactics or weapons—in order to fight the

Spaniards in Cuba? General officers and colonels who had been commissioned before the Civil War were the most resentful. One man led his force on maneuvers in 1904 by, according to one observer, merely becoming enraged and spouting profanities. Another, an artillerist, was prevented from firing his gun by safety officers for being so helpless. These officers opposed Root: men usually of meager verbal resources but of equivalent cunning and tenacity in their efforts to thwart reform. In the verbiage of twenty-first-century politicians, these officers were akin to the most obstructing of federal bureaucrats.

Root was a serious and determined student of American and European military history, and he concluded that the United States should have a *general staff*, that its head, or chief, should answer directly to the secretary of war, that he should be hired and sustained in office at the secretary's pleasure, and that he should be the secretary's principal military adviser. His staff would furnish the materials necessary to make needed decisions; above all this staff would plan for contingencies and begin to function as a co-coordinative agency for the various elements of the War Department.

Root's general staff proposal was not approved and enacted into law until 1903. Meantime, on his own initiative, he had created, with the support of several mid-rank officers in the war secretary's own staff, an Army War College, which would become the planning heart of the general staff: a college in the sense of a "collegium," a body of trained planners relieved of other day-to-day duties. This general staff, and the primacy of the chief of staff as uniformed head of the army, would not realize their full maturity until the end of World War I; once realized, however, it became the primary agency of army planning and command. Twenty years later, in the 1939–1945 war, Marshall's authority in the army would be supreme and unchallenged.

Among the most important of the Root reforms was his rationalization of the troubled, inchoate relationship between the regular army and the American citizen soldiery who had been, and would always have to be, summoned to the colors in time of war: in a word, the militia. Like the word "tuition," the term "militia" was employed with imprecision. It could mean the whole able-bodied male population of the United States, or it could mean National Guard units maintained by the states—units that under certain circumstances might be called to active duty for limited periods of time. It could imply volunteers summoned for emergencies, or retired soldiers. The states were jealous of their prerogatives: they wished to control their National Guard units, to prescribe their duties and the limits upon them. Their representatives in Congress were zealous partisans on their behalf. It was in the rationalization of this troubled relationship between National Guard and regulars that Root, in effect, reorganized the structure of the army, with the consequence that the position of chief of staff became the effective head—CEO—of the army.

Another noted reform of Root's tenure was a requirement that all company-grade officers of less than ten years' active service attend "garrison school" for at least ninety days a year. Root believed in education—practical, focused education of the kind that young officers who had fought in the war against Spain and during the Philippines insurrection had so conspicuously lacked. Other things being equal, Root wrote that officers who kept their minds alert intellectually and studied those difficulties that they were likely to eventually encounter would be the stronger practical men and better soldiers. Most of the younger officers would have agreed, but with the reservation that a certain disjunction would always distinguish professional *education* from the *training* necessary to ensure that an officer uses his education to useful advantage. Training implies indoctrination, habituation, the inculcation of qualities of "character." Military men have tended to see in education a certain dissolvent effect. The pale cast of thought tends to chasten the native hue of resolution. Root was determined both to overcome such prejudices and to ensure that young officers knew the elements of their profession. Marshall was among the earliest beneficiaries of Root's reforms.

Like the best cabinet officers, Root knew when to leave. He had attended to the duties for which President McKinley had hired him—those of administration and policy. But these were not the absorbing missions of his tenure. Beginning with a plain understanding of what an American army needed to be, and a patient but unerring sense of the initiatives and policies that might serve that

end, he had undertaken and largely carried through policies of reform. These reforms of military education, command and control, and the relations between regulars and
reserves were controverted and thwarted by opponents
determined to secure their own comfortable patterns of
authority and labor, but they would nevertheless be realized within fifteen years of his departure, on February 1,
1904, from the War Department. Encomia were sincere
and plentiful: the British war secretary Lord Richard
Haldane was known to have believed that Root's five
annual reports were authorities on the place of an army
in a democracy. Root's colleague John Hay and other
friends likewise remarked that Root was distinguished
for his disinterestedness and exceptional character.

The Root reforms were profoundly diffusive in their
consequences, but the turf wars and battles they would
engender continued for many years. Not until General
Peyton C. March became chief of staff (1918–1921) did
the general staff become the dominant planning agency
Root had envisaged, and not until then were the various
bureaus brought fully under firm control of the chief of
staff. Along with the final adjustment in relations among
the various active and reserve components of the army,
and the full vitalization of the army's educational programs, these changes constitute Root's legacy to the War
Department and the army, and by extension, American
people.

Much less remarked is a certain spiritual consanguinity with Henry Stimson, Elihu Root's younger

law partner and later secretary of war (twice), and with George Marshall. Marshall, particularly, deployed the same resources of character and temperament that distinguished Root: granitic resolution. This was a determination importantly, patiently, and quietly used. It was tactfully employed and willing to give way on small things to achieve larger purposes—qualities extolled repeatedly in Marshall's letters (as in Abraham Lincoln's). Neither great leader was especially concerned with public approval. Each also was a master in his dealings with Congress.

. . .

In 1904, success in garrison school at Fort Reno was earned mainly by memorizing scattered sections of a few "set" texts, and by regular attendance at classes offered once or twice a week. While Marshall discharged the untaxing duties of garrison life, mastered his assigned texts, and, with Lily, enjoyed the raw countryside and magnificent vistas thereabouts, he hoped for an assignment to the Infantry and Cavalry School at Fort Leavenworth—to which, there being no other candidate from Fort Reno in 1906, he was finally seconded that summer. There was a serendipity in the timing of Marshall's appointment. The new chief of staff of the army, Major General J. Franklin Bell, had just left Leavenworth, where he had been commandant. Bell's interest in the schools remained avid, however, and as chief of staff, he worried that too many posts were assigning young officers to Leavenworth simply as a means of getting the less talented out of the way. Thus, he ordered that no officer below the grade of captain be accepted. Marshall made the cut by less than a year. It was an assignment, seen in retrospect, from which the rest of his career flowed. It was here he began to build the foundation of a most singular reputation.

Chapter Five

Fort Leavenworth

Marshall and Lily left Fort Reno in the summer of 1906—Marshall to report to Fort Leavenworth, Lily to return to Virginia until married quarters were available at Leavenworth. He now joined a class of fifty-four officers, of which he was most junior. In 1907, the course would be renamed the "Army School of the Line."[1] Its purpose was to teach those subjects with which all company-grade officers must be familiar. Success in the course—graduating among the top 50 percent—assured retention at Leavenworth for a year-long assignment at the Army Staff College afterward.

The army had been hostile to Bell's revival of Leavenworth. It was called "Bell's Folly," the military suspicion of "education" immediately asserting itself. This attitude would change as the graduates of the schools began to distinguish themselves in the First World War: nine members of Marshall's class would become general officers during the war or afterward.

These dynamics had no effect on student culture in Marshall's class. Gossip identified several officers, all senior to Marshall, as prospective highfliers. These were men who would lead the class. It disclosed, also, that some officers had been coached for the curriculum ahead, and that they had copies of the previous year's tactical problems. Marshall's reaction, not unlike his response to hearing Stuart argue that he should not be permitted to attend VMI, was to commit himself to *leading* his class—which, in an academic culture that measured grades down to the hundredths, he did. "The competition was intense, but I always felt it was a good thing, because the officers that under a strain got rattled did exactly the same thing when they got into battle," Marshall recalled.[2]

At the Staff College, Marshall was exposed to a remarkable teacher: Major John F. Morrison. Morrison was an army intellectual of a familiar but uncommon type, a teacher who cast a longer intellectual shadow over the young officers who passed through Leavenworth than any professor before (or likely since), and whose peculiar gifts suited him ideally to his duties. He was bulky and clumsy, socially diffident, a Johnsonian character with the great pedagogue's strange ignorance of his own effect on others. Morrison was an early champion of what a later age would call the case system: military tactics, he believed, were to be learned not by memorizing principles or cultivating an ability to regurgitate what was taught but by meticulous analysis of individual tactical situations, most selected from after-action reports of campaigns and battles in the Franco-Prussian War (1870–1871). The student was expected to learn essential principles, through the elemental issues presented by each situation. Little more than a decade later, Marshall and his contemporaries, many of them former students or teachers at Leavenworth, were amazed to find themselves serving in venues and fighting for objectives that Morrison's maps had made familiar. Captain Fox Conner, an artillerist who would become John Pershing's chief of operations in France, remembered his reliance on maps first encountered at Leavenworth: "The maps he used [in the Great War] were the very ones he had complained about in his student days."[3]

Marshall and Lily lived quietly at Fort Leavenworth, avoiding socializing by pleading, a trifle disingenuously, that Lily's heart condition required a life without excitement or stress. Marshall was now beginning to discover in himself an aptitude for what it was soldiers were expected to know how to do. For the better part of a year, Marshall labored away, working late into the evenings, allowing spare time only for preparation for the examinations required for promotion to first lieutenant, during the 1906–1907 winter holidays.[4] At the end of the first-year course, Marshall was ranked first in his class, and at the end of the Staff College year, in 1908, he was selected—the junior man by far—to remain at the school as an instructor in the Department of Engineering and Military Arts. In his assessment, it was said that Marshall was exceptionally capable and valuable to both departments and that his services were greatly needed. J. Franklin Bell, now chief of staff of the army and formerly head of the Leavenworth schools, approved the appointment with enthusiasm.

. . .

Marshall's successes at Leavenworth were less the consequence of blossoming talent as of a tautly focused disciplining of an ordinary human capability: that of being able to concentrate, in solitude, for long periods, on an essential to be mastered. It is a quality that exists at the intersection of intellect and "character." It has little to do with IQ, but it habituates the mind to things in context, to considering consequences, to the development of prudence. Marshall in his first years of serious reflection on his profession—at Leavenworth, from 1906 to 1910—was preparing and educating such a mind. In World War II, he would stun those who watched him by an ability, continually on display, to deploy large amounts of learned information (facts, names, orders, et cetera), in an unhurried, seemingly effortless fashion. He was always clear in his oral and written communications. In the Second World War, on occasion, he would solicit questions from forty or fifty reporters gathered for an interview, and then, all questions having been asked, respond to each in the order it had been posed. This was done without parade or condescension. "I learned how to learn," Marshall said of his years at Leavenworth.[5] Like his future protégé Dwight D. Eisenhower, a schoolboy in another part of Kansas while Marshall was learning and teaching at Leavenworth, he proved himself to have been, at VMI, not so much an indifferent student as an unengaged one. Like those of most successful American generals, his powers of intellection would prove to have been developed after college. Nineteen years later, Eisenhower would also finish first in his class at Leavenworth.

The consequence of this cultivated capability—to fix attention on what must be mastered—was a mind scouring away all extrinsic influences, all solicitations of competing duties, all vagrant ruminations. Functional austerity was the result. It would be the quality of mind colleagues and superiors would note in Marshall to the end of his career. Again: this was not an early blossoming of an intellectual "gift" but rather the identification of an ordinary capability that must be schooled and disciplined to serve purposively.

Marshall had made two important discoveries by this time: first, that academic success at Leavenworth had not been a matter of cleverness and verbal facility. He had discovered at Leavenworth that he could make his mind a retentive instrument and could hold many data that would suggest, shape, and precipitate on a "solution." Second, Marshall's ambition provided him with a sustaining fuel, an ambition to excel, to stand out, to demonstrate to his classmates that, green and disregarded as he may have been, he could match and surpass them. Again it was—as his official biographer suggested—the chance overhearing of comments perhaps dismissive of his abilities that provoked and sustained his ambition.

.   .   .

In 1908, two years after Marshall had begun his studies at Fort Leavenworth, a senior infantry captain was being shown around the post. The captain was himself to begin the same courses that fall. The officer's escort pointed to a student sitting in the front row: "The wizard of this class is that rangy youngster down there.... He is a brand new first lieutenant by the name of George C. Marshall."[6]

John McAuley Palmer had been detailed to the School of the Line from his own post, a member of the second class into which no one below the grade of captain was eligible to be admitted. In the fall, he discovered that Lieutenant Marshall, the rangy youngster, was now a member of the faculty. There were two other officers on post somewhat junior to Palmer: Douglas MacArthur and Walter Krueger, both lieutenants with faculty appointments. "The very idea of being subordinate to such youngsters came as something of a shock to senior officers as conscious of their dignity as we were," he recalled.[7]

Palmer and Marshall were to become lifelong friends. Seniority in grade soon came to mean very little. Palmer's is among the earliest testimonials to Marshall's standing and reputation in a setting in which hard thinking—

thinking of a particular kind—was the criterion of progress and distinction.

In the year following his meeting Palmer, in the
summer of 1909, Marshall left Leavenworth on three
months' leave. He and Lily spent most of this time in
Virginia and among Lily's kinfolk in Albemarle County.
The following year, in September 1910, they left the
United States for five months' travel in Britain and on
the Continent. In those unhurried days, such absences
from military duty were not unusual. Exemplary exhaustion from continuous overwork had not yet become
the insignia of professional soldiering. The last part of
the five months' furlough had in fact been an extension of Marshall's leave, approved by Ulysses Grant's
son, Major General Frederick D. Grant, USMA class
of 1871, "in order to enable Lieutenant Marshall to take
full advantage of his trip to Europe." He did: Marshall
and Lily visited in Austria, France, Italy; they toured
cities, cathedrals, museums, castles, galleries, gratifying a
thirst, typical for Americans of the time, to see the Old
World. Marshall also managed to see something of the
British Army. Denied permission to accompany units
on maneuver near Aldershot as an observer, he rented a
bike in a village and, with a notebook and field glasses,
followed along on his own.

Chapter Six

Lieutenant and Captain

An early biographer, Robert Payne, called certain incidents in the long years of Marshall's lieutenancy—as recalled by contemporaries decades later—the early miracles of a saint. Two occurred in the Philippines: one was trivial, the other perhaps portentous. In the first, Marshall made a small wager with another officer that, at an inspection of his company that day, the inspecting officer would fail to note three important failures in the unit's tactical demonstration but would pounce upon three minor shortcomings of appearance in ranks. The bet was won, and Marshall collected. Marshall had precisely predicted the in-ranks errors: a poor shave, a button not fastened on a soldier's tunic, a missing bayonet in another's scabbard. The former Leavenworth instructor in tactics was far less interested in "appearance" than in evidence of operational proficiency: his point was that too many peacetime garrison officers were obsessed with such minutiae.

One of Marshall's commanding officers would make the notation, years later, that Marshall supplied an unusual "example of a soldier whose military genius was cultivated and grew in peacetime." If this was true, it was the singular circumstance of service in a large-scale maneuver in the Philippines, and a few others like it, that furnished the opportunity for such growth.

In the years between 1905 and 1913, Japanese-American relations had grown distinctly wary, with the consequence that American soldiers in the Philippines had begun to see Japan as a possible invading power. She had won a mammoth victory over Russia in 1905, had taken over Korea five years later, had continued to build and train a regular army far larger than what was needed for homeland defense. Japan was now the strongest naval power in the Pacific. War between the United States and Japan was unlikely but not unthinkable, and in this circumstance, General Bell decided to undertake large-scale maneuvers of his forces. Almost five thousand soldiers were to assemble on the southern coast of Luzon, at Batangas Bay, their mission to march on Manila, a hundred miles north. They were to defeat a defending army half their size, already established in positions prepared and occupied beforehand.

Marshall was assigned as adjutant to the invading White Force. Three days before its assembly, the component units received their alerts and orders to proceed to Batangas Bay—some by forced march, others by boat. At this point, the colonel commanding the White Force gave final proof that he was unable to do his duty. Like most of his contemporaries, given army practices of promotion by seniority only, he had neither the energy nor the endurance to lead such an operation in the fierce humidity and heat of a Philippine summer. He rode in a wagon, not on horseback, and, according to Marshall, repeatedly "refreshed himself against the Philippine heat" from the contents of a flask. Marshall argued that the old duffer should *not* be relieved; a new man, all circumstances considered, might be worse. He was allowed to remain. Meantime, the colonel's own chief of staff became sick and had to be removed. A liaison officer in General Bell's confidence nominated Marshall to replace him. Bell concurred, and now Lieutenant Marshall was, in effect, commanding the 4,800-man attacking force.

Marshall embraced his new responsibilities with a palpable efficiency, with a demonstrated mastery over all elements of the maneuver force's operations, particularly the coordination among its various units, that those who watched him never forgot. He proved singularly resourceful, also: the maneuver was not designed as a "set piece" demonstration. Constant changes, most of them involving fresh difficulties, faulty intelligence, poor communications, et cetera, were introduced by the supervisors and umpires. Marshall was equal to them all. The most vivid memory of this prodigy of improvised command was recorded by another lieutenant, Henry H. Arnold, USMA class of 1907, who happened to be standing in a jungle clearing while Marshall, seated on the ground with his maps and notes before him, dictated comprehensive and detailed orders for the day's attacks by the various White Force units. Arnold never forgot what he heard and saw, and he immediately "wrote his wife that he had just seen a future Chief of Staff in action."[1]

The enterprise was ended a week later. Manila was saved, and after-action reports were unstinting in their praise of Lieutenant Marshall's work. For his part, Marshall would now pay a price—the first of several such bills to come due—of complete nervous and physical exhaustion. He spent two weeks in the hospital recovering strength, was granted two months' leave, later extended by another eight weeks. (He made use of the extension to visit Japan, and later, the sites of Japan's successful campaigns in Manchuria during its late victory over Russia). His notes and observations on the war and on the Japanese army, fleshed out and organized, became the basis for the lectures he delivered later.

It had been a memorable performance. It was evidence, if any were needed, of an *integrative* habit of mind—a capability that had been cultivated and trained and *made* habitual. Marshall had developed a way of organizing unrelated data in his mind and then ordering them according to the need presented by the situation. Marshall would provide many examples of this kind of capability in both world wars, particularly in the mobilization and organization of the army in the early 1940s, and later, as secretary of state.

This sort of capability distinguishes many "great commanders." In many ways, it is a distant but recognizable relative of the ability to solve, without strain, elementary problems in algebra—trains moving at different speeds from different starting points, et cetera, in which students must calculate times of arrival, collision, and the like. Allowances being made for the unusual training Marshall had both offered and undergone at Leavenworth and on maneuvers in the United States, the Philippines maneuver of 1914 was a prodigy. This was soon known as such, throughout the army. Marshall's company was now ordered to duty on Corregidor, but Marshall was again detached as an "aide," this time to another general officer newly arrived in the islands, Hunter Liggett, whom Marshall (as a second lieutenant) had tutored at Leavenworth. Among other things, he was assigned to work on plans for the defense of Manila—against the prospective enemy, Japan, this time from the north, from the Lingayen Gulf. This was precisely where a strong Japanese task force would land one day: December 22, 1941. Liggett admired Marshall's work; they would find themselves working together again, not in the Philippines, but much sooner than either could have imagined. This opportunity came in France, in the Great War.

.   .   .

More than any American soldier, Robert E. Lee and George Washington excepted, Marshall invites the comfortable imputation that he was always the soldier whom the world came to know in his maturity: forbearing, calm, selfless, wise, dutiful, disinterested. But becoming *that* Marshall was the self-supervised labor of many years. Like Lee and Washington, he both suppressed and hid vagrant ambitions and impulses that, he knew, would disserve his ambition and his colleagues' continuing admiration of what he permitted them to see of himself. However hidden, that ambition was both potent and unassuageable, and it delighted both in its triumphs and in testimonials to its successes. Marshall, that is to say, was a normal (in one sense) young professional army officer. An extended excerpt from a letter he wrote to his older brother, Stuart, whom he seldom wrote but whom, clearly, he wanted to impress, makes the point. He describes his role in the Batangas maneuvers:

> Between you and myself I had an opportunity that rarely ever comes to a Colonel, and has never been heard of before being given to anyone below that rank, except General Pershing—he was then 42 years old and a senior captain. I had absolute command and control of the Detachment, appointed even the adjutant and aides. The Colonel was ignored by General Bell . . . but they wouldn't relieve him from supposed command during the maneuvers as they did not want a more assertive Colonel to . . . relieve me of actual control. . . . You must treat as really confidential . . . what I tell you . . . *I trust you will read this to yourself*

*tear it up and disabuse your mind of the idea that I am
rather a remarkable braggart.* I don't tell you things
about myself—successes—but this one was rather
unique and unheard of during peacetimes. . . . [2]

A little more than a year later, only nine months
before his return to the United States, Marshall wrote a
long letter to his former mathematics instructor at VMI,
Edward Nichols, now superintendent at the institute,
who had become a sympathetic correspondent and
admirer. Like Scott Shipp, who had died in 1917, and like
many college presidents of an earlier time, he kept careful
tabs on the careers of his ablest graduates. Nichols had
twice tried to secure Marshall's services as commandant,
an attractive situation both for Marshall and Lily. Marshall declined. The timing wasn't right—it never would
be; nor, he surely understood, would the assignment have
been useful to his army career.

His letter to Nichols is of a familiar type: the young
soldier (or priest or teacher) confides frustration about
the progress of his career. He is no longer young. He is
conscious of an unusual ability and a honed aptitude
for the work of his profession, and though these have
been acknowledged by his superiors, there have been
no palpable rewards. Useful recognitions were missing.
The letter has an enjambed, gossipy cast—the kind that
signals to its reader that something more serious is coming. Marshall reported on the son of an alumnus who
was an applicant for admission to the institute; he made

a perfunctory observation about "Mrs. Marshall," who
had just returned from Japan, where she went "for the
clothes." Then, suddenly:

> The absolute stagnation in promotion has caused
> me to make tentative plans for resigning as soon as
> business conditions improve. . . . [It is not] right to
> waste all my best years in the vain struggle against
> insurmountable obstacles.

But this was no cri de coeur. Conceivably (though we
cannot know this), it was prompted by Lily or by some
incident that was not mentioned. Essentially, it was a
young man's request for reassurance and counsel. Nichols
provided it: "You are an eminent success in your present line of endeavor, highly esteemed by everyone who
knows you and with a standing in the service of the
very highest. . . . I am sure in time you will be among the
high ranking officers in the service."[3] Nichols reminded
Marshall that the army was planning an increase in size,
although he made no mention of tensions with Mexico
and a concentration of American forces on the Mexican
border. Similarly, he made no mention at all of a possible American entry into the war in Europe. (The letter
was written some seven months after the sinking of the
Lusitania on May 7, 1915.)

In the closed-tight culture of the army officer corps
between the war with Spain and World War I, satisfactions and a sense of fulfillment were not to be gained

from promotion, from money, from (even) decorations. Robert E. Lee—along with Benjamin Franklin, one of Marshall's acknowledged heroes—urged the soldier of his defeated Army of Northern Virginia to take satisfaction from consciousness of duty performed. Modern scholarship assigns the drafting of the famous order to Lee's aide Charles Marshall, a cousin of Lieutenant George C. Marshall—who, like any talented person of reasonable ambition, would for a while have to glean his satisfaction in the same way.

All this was about to change, however, and abruptly.

.   .   .

Considered together, the years and assignments of George Marshall's career between his first tour of duty in the Philippines (1902–1903) and his departure from the islands not long after his letter to Nichols—these years are distinguished for two things. First, Marshall had a range and character of assignments that seem fitted perfectly as a means of preparing him for the nature of his later service. Second, Marshall developed a schooled aptitude for military service that was consistently noted by those for whom, and with whom, he worked. This aptitude was severely functional in execution. It was the consequence of a cold and methodical ardor to master the rudiments of the military profession. It was undramatic, unremittingly competitive, and dutiful. By the end of the period, Marshall was still a first lieutenant (though he would be promoted to captain shortly), but he was recognized throughout the army as one of the two ablest officers of his generation. And the contrast with the other, Douglas MacArthur, could not have been more stark.

Three months after his return from the Philippines, Marshall was promoted to captain: October 13, 1916. By this point, he had already been denied the assignment he wanted and expected—service with Brigadier General John Pershing's expedition into Mexico to find and bring to justice the rebel Pancho Villa. Nevertheless, General Bell retained Marshall as an aide, with station at the Presidio of San Francisco, but now with a new mission: preparing prospective officers for possible active service—should the Woodrow Wilson administration find it necessary to summon a national army to augment regular forces and National Guard. War had broken out in Europe in 1914; the *Lusitania* had been sunk with more than 120 Americans killed. The regular army, now comprising only 5,175 officers and 103,224 enlisted men, was plainly unready, ill-equipped, and undermanned.[4] However reluctantly, President Wilson endorsed "preparedness."

General Bell was now head of the Western Department, responsible for two of the volunteer training camps that the army had organized around the country. Younger businessmen and other professionals attended these encampments for six weeks—at their own expense, subjecting themselves to a mild regimen of military training in the most basic usages of the profession. The idea had been current for three years at least—the camps' earliest models, in the northeast, had been organized by university presidents with the enthusiastic backing of Army Chief of Staff Leonard Wood and various alumni of Theodore Roosevelt's Rough Riders. From the beginning, these "Plattsburg" camps (so-named after the first of the businessmen's camps, in upstate New York) attracted the *ton* of New York, Boston, and Philadelphia society: graduates of Harvard, Columbia, Yale, et cetera. These men were Anglophiles, bred in a culture that endorsed strenuous, manly pursuits and tests of physical courage, and who saw military service—should war occur—as both rite of passage and patriotic obligation.

Bell immediately sent Marshall to help Major General William Sibert with his training camp at Monterey, California. As always it was understood already that Marshall's assignment as an "aide" did not imply the duties usually given aides. Rather, he was to serve as a kind of factotum and adviser to his general (Liggett, Bell, Sibert, and later, Pershing). This simultaneously comforted and confused the generals and colonels whom Marshall was sent out to "help." Ordinarily, the gaining general was grateful; Sibert, for example, asked for Marshall to be assigned to his staff a year later when he, Sibert, was ordered to command the First Infantry Division being assembled for duty in France.

Bell sent Marshall to study the camp at Monterey. Again, this implied that Marshall was to offer assistance to the camp commandant, to suggest improvements in the program. What he found was bizarre: the "camp" was laid out on the grounds of the Hotel Del Monte, an oasis of privilege, glamour, "luxury and wealth ... and decaying idealism."[5] Marshall attached himself initially to a company of volunteers; observing, making suggestions, eventually taking charge of their training. A few days later, Sibert reassigned him to another company and repeated the procedure until Marshall had made the rounds. Occasionally Marshall chastised and exhorted:

> "You fellows came down here because you were enthusiastic to do something in this time of emergency. ... This morning you were ... in reserve, sitting around and resting ... your wives and girls brought out good things and you had champagne and it has been quite delightful to sit out under the trees. Now you are so exhausted from this war service you can't do a damn thing."[6]

Marshall then drilled the men, hard, for several hours. He made additional demands of them and was soon everywhere in the camp, earning for himself the nickname "Dynamite" Marshall. Marshall soon repeated the performance at another volunteer camp in Utah, Fort Douglas, but this marked the effective end of less than purposive duty. His service at Fort Douglas elicited an efficiency report that Forrest Pogue called "perhaps that the most extraordinary praise any Army officer ever had in ... routine efficiency reports on which promotion is based."[7]

To the formulaic inquiry—"Would you like to have this officer serving in your command?"—Lieutenant Colonel Johnson Hagood responded: "Yes, but I would prefer to serve *under his command*.... [He is] a military genius [and should] be made a brigadier general in the regular Army, and every day this is postponed is a loss to the Army and the nation."[8]

.　　.　　.

Following Germany's resumption of unrestricted submarine warfare on February 1, 1917, the sinking of several more American ships, and the discovery of a telegram from the German foreign minister (to the president of Mexico) promising, in exchange for an alliance with Mexico, the return to her of Arizona, New Mexico, and other territories lost to the United States in the Mexican War, President Wilson asked Congress for a declaration of war. It was granted on April 6, 1917. In the consequent reshuffle of senior officers, Bell was reassigned as commanding general of the Eastern Department, in New York. Marshall and Lily moved cross-country to take up new duties. But the elderly Bell, like the superannuated colonel in the Philippine maneuvers, suddenly became incapacitated. Marshall, the aide-de-camp, was now the effective commander of a department. As the saying goes, history may indeed repeat itself.

Marshall was obliged to act as Bell's deputy and executive officer both, guarding the secrets of Bell's illness and his whereabouts, issuing orders and fielding requests in the general's name.[9] Marshall was at the center of an urgent clamor: state and local politicians, old friends of Bell's, Wall Street tycoons, et cetera, all demanded appointments to the officers' training camps, appointments to direct commissions, or orders to join the army in France. Unsatisfied with Marshall's anodyne and patient responses, they demanded to speak to the general—who, fearlessly brave in battle, was fearful that, if word got out about his hospitalization, it would ruin whatever chance he had of commanding a division in France. Late each afternoon, Marshall would visit him, make a full report, receive his orders, and return to his office.

Marshall was responsible for ensuring that the officers' camps were ready for the officer candidates assigned to them; for denying the unending demands of important New Yorkers for preferential treatment (but for admirable motives: they wanted to get into uniform, get commissions, and fight); for running departmental headquarters. All the while, Marshall sought assignment for overseas service himself. General George Washington, when he hired the young Alexander Hamilton as an aide, wrote that he required someone who could "comprehend at one view the diversity of the matter, which comes before me, so as to afford the ready assistance, which every man in my situation must stand more or less in need of." "It is absolutely necessary," he later continued, "for me to have persons that can think for me, as well as execute orders."[10] These were the services Marshall was providing Bell.

Marshall was desperate to serve in France. General Bell was willing to oblige him with a recommendation, but the newly appointed commander of the American Expeditionary Forces (AEF), John Pershing, was reluctant to deprive Bell, a former chief of staff, of his principal aide. So Marshall endured the agony of watching Pershing and his entourage pass through Bell's New York headquarters before boarding the SS *Baltic* in harbor on May 28, 1917. Most were in ill-fitting civilian clothes. It was raining, and they presented a singularly unprepossessing spectacle. Lily Marshall observed: "What a miserable-looking set of men they were." The silly idea was, if the *Baltic* were torpedoed, the men might be taken for civilians.

It is unclear how Marshall finally secured his appointment. Perhaps it was through the offices of General Nichols, to whom he had sent recent efficiency reports, all of them embarrassingly laudatory, including Hagood's. Another hypothesis points to the intervention of General William Sibert, whom he had helped at the Monterey camp. Or, just maybe, it was Bell himself. But the appointment did arrive—in the form of a request on June 3—in a telegram from Sibert, who had been selected to command the division now being assembled as the first American unit to be sent to France.

Among Marshall's last duties at General Bell's headquarters was responding to a request from several newly married second lieutenants, all fresh graduates of one of the officers' camps, for a day's honeymoon leave before they sailed for France. He approved them all. Much later, Marshall recalled, he learned they had all been killed in the fighting.

Marshall arranged for Lily to join her mother in Charlotte, North Carolina, and by the night of June 10, 1917, he had joined the First Division, which then boarded a flotilla of army transports in Hoboken, New Jersey. He was to be the division's assistant chief of staff (for operations), joining, on the lead vessel *Tenadores,* two contemporaries who would figure importantly in his life much later: Lesley McNair (USMA class of 1904), assigned as division training officer, and Major Frank R. McCoy (USMA class of 1897), on his way to join Pershing's staff. Neither McNair nor Marshall had any illusions about the tasks before them; the reform of the military under Root providing but a lesser disadvantage. The First Division was as ill prepared for war as any of Ulysses S. Grant's volunteer regiments brought together before the Battle of Shiloh. Perhaps worse. Comprising four regiments of infantry, none with a full complement of soldiers or officers, none with any experience of coordinated action in campaigning or in battle, the First Division was only a designation. The regiments had been fleshed out, en route from their assignments along the Texas border, with soldiers and new recruits from other units. Many of them were given their rifles as they boarded trains north; the army was little further advanced in its ability to mobilize than it had been in 1898. One regimental history—the Eighteenth Infantry's—later admitted that it had just made itself into a "strange organization that had never existed before in the U.S."[11] But the important thing was that the United States, the president yielding to Marshal Joseph Joffre's fervent appeals, had moved beyond a simple acknowledgment of belligerency in its declaration of war. It was now sending, as an earnest reflection of its determination to do its share, a full division of soldiers—some twenty-five thousand men—to train and to fight in France. It was certain that, as soon as the division, the ancestor of the famous Big Red One, took its first casualties, their country would respond with angry, stouthearted enthusiasm to the need to send more.

By the time the guns fell silent on the western front seventeen months later, two million doughboys would be in France. In the last six weeks of their active wartime service, twenty-six thousand would be killed in battle.

.   .   .

From the time of his commissioning until the date of his departure for Europe—fifteen years, five months—Marshall had been the beneficiary both of chronology and of a singular admixture of qualities of character, mind, and temperament. As Colonel Hagood had observed, Marshall had already furnished an example of military genius declaring itself in *peacetime.* It was a peculiar kind of military genius: a manufactured aptness, a cultivated ability to do, efficiently, without exciting envy or resentment, those things that the evolving American army of the prewar period required. It was a military aptitude both the product of, and perfectly suited to, the need of a commercial, democratic republic, of a country that could be "military" when provoked but which hated the usages of militarism and the pretensions of military culture. Its purest expression, all things considered, was its mobilization, deployment, and fighting quality of soldiers recruited and volunteered for the Splendid Little War against Spain. As an American statesman would observe forty years later, Americans wanted to win quickly, come home, drink Coke, and go to the movies.

Marshall understood how to lead citizen soldiers produced by such a culture. He had made himself a student of his profession. He had been given large responsibilities in circumstances of isolation, those that demanded above all self-reliance of execution. These circumstances carried no particular expectation of promotion, decoration, or celebrity—or material reward. His collateral ancestor Charles Marshall, thought to have drafted Lee's *Farewell Address to the Army of Northern Virginia,* identified its only, but transcendent, reward: the satisfaction of duty fulfilled. Marshall had brought himself, made himself, the servitor to such an ethos. He would now test it, test himself, on a much larger stage.

Chapter Seven

First World War

The First World War retains only a weak—
and faltering—purchase on American sensibilities
and memories. It seems an ancient horror, mammoth
and terrible, but impossibly distant. The numbers of dead
stun and overwhelm; they no longer kindle outrage or
pity. "The infinite spaces/Are still silent . . . History, even,
does not know what is meant."[1] Guernica, Auschwitz,
Pearl Harbor, Dresden, and Hiroshima have intervened.
So have Vietnam and September 11. An American generation born in 1980 is a generation of great-grandchildren
of the Great War's dwindling cohort of survivors. The
battlefields of France that Americans visit are almost
always those of a later war.

It is equally difficult to evoke the character of Franco-
American friendship of that time: a friendship that was
passionate and tender—and fraternal. The embrace of
the two countries that followed the American declaration of war on Germany (April 6, 1917, thirty-two months

after the war had begun), was both celebrated and felt as the embrace of old allies, of two *republics*. The French marshal Joseph Joffre's mission to Washington, just after the declaration, aimed to secure an early commitment of American soldiers to the fighting. Joffre, a great jolly clot of a man, succeeded immediately. A full division was to be assembled and shipped across the Atlantic as soon as possible. Draft legislation was prepared and enacted on May 18, 1917. Major General John Pershing, meantime, with a scratch staff, sailed from New York Harbor on the *Baltic* on May 28, arriving in Paris on June 13. The party was welcomed with ceremonies at Les Invalides, where Pershing kissed the hilt of a sword of Napoleon's, and an aide, fluent in French, concluded proper remarks with the inspiration of the moment: "La Fayette, nous voilà!"

.   .   .

The narrative of how Marshall and what was now called the First Division came to be in eastern France in November 1917 is essentially the narrative of the American entry into the war, and of the American Expeditionary Forces' early service in France.

On a dank warm evening, June 14, 1917, Marshall watched the last of the soldiers assigned to the *Tenadores* make their way up its narrow gangway. "We are watching a harvest of death," one of the interested onlookers confided in him. (As it turns out, this was an accurate prognostication.) The *Tenadores* slipped quietly through the Narrows, out toward the Atlantic, toward France, and, most important, toward war. Only a few muffled sounds would have bruised the silence: a foghorn perhaps, a tug's engine. Marshall rarely mused about the significance of such moments. Still, we may impute to him a soldier's grateful consciousness of an end of training and preparation for more service. The disjunction between such soldiering and wartime is total. Marshall would now cross over. Like the young narrator in *A Dance to the Music of Time,* Marshall could not have failed to note that this was one of those passages that occur in a lifetime. Marshall's mission on the trip across, and in the first months in France, was to help General Sibert create a fighting division out of the chaos of an unprepared American army.

For whatever his pride about beginning his service in France, Marshall was soon to be overwhelmed by the palpable sense of grief, the lifeless expressions on the faces of the men and women he saw. Most of the women were in black. The townspeople trudged about in attitudes of bleak resignation. "Everyone seemed to be on the verge of tears."[2] The young men of the town had absorbed terrible casualties; the other soldiers who had passed through the port, Canadians, earlier in the war, had meant nothing to its resolution. Marshall, trying out his VMI French, engaged a longshoreman: *"Je suis très beau aujoud'hui* [sic]."[3] "Thereafter," Marshall wrote, "I never spoke French unless forced to do so."

French witnesses found the Americans' appearance, these early representatives of an army that would grow to two million, overwhelming. This was not so much due to the fact that they were, at last, here, but rather caused by the character of their appearance: what they looked like. Months later, Vera Brittain watched them marching toward some unknown front:

> At first I thought their spruce clean uniforms were those of officers ... they looked larger than ordinary men; their tall, straight figures were in vivid contrast to the undersized armies of pale recruits to which we had grown accustomed ... they seemed, as it were, Tommies in heaven. . . . I watched them move with such rhythm, such dignity, such serene consciousness and self-respect.[4]

A battalion-size contingent of First Division men was hastily assembled to march in a July Fourth parade on the Champs-Élysées. The unit's officers were in a terrible fret about the rawness of the young soldiers, the absence of drilled precision and snap in their marching, and the sloppy cut of their uniforms. In their innocence, though, to the French, they appeared in their limber athleticism, their carefree swinging gait, to be the embodiment of what they had imagined American soldiers must be like. A story circulated, its effect not so much to shock as to charm. A great French general had visited the temporary headquarters of the First Division soon after its debarkation at Saint-Nazaire. He climbed out of his limousine, idly watched by an American private supposedly standing guard. The soldier was a lanky Tennessean, sloppily accoutred in an ill-fitting unbuttoned blouse, with a watch chain strung between its breast pockets. He did not salute. The general, assuming the soldier had no idea who or what he was, gestured affably: *Let me see your rifle, son.* The man handed it over and withdrew to a window ledge; he busied himself in rolling a cigarette. Marshall set the boy straight. He speculated later that the soldier most likely fought bravely and was among those killed in one of the great battles of 1918.

Stories such as these were received as evidences of buoyant and unjaded strength and promise. Given proper leadership, Pershing was certain, such human material would triumph. He confided an amateur's anthropological explanation, one that George Patton would endorse in another war twenty-five years later: the immigrants and their progeny who had come to the New World "had the willpower and spirit to seek opportunity . . . rather than put up with unbearable conditions in the old [world] . . . we had developed a manhood superior in initiative to that existing abroad, which given approximately equal training and discipline, developed a superior soldier."[5] George Marshall's recollection, twenty years later, was vivid—and anguished. The United States, trusting some primordial if nameless quality in its character believed it could improvise armies overnight, that the young citizens who would answer the call were the beneficiaries of a history and culture that made them natural fighting men. They would always serve a moral cause—and this itself would ensure their ardor and bravery.

.   .   .

American grand strategy in the Great War was dictated not by the circumstances that had led to Congress's declaration of war but by the requirement to rouse and sustain full-throated American support for American arms *in* the war. This meant that boasting of a large American army in France in turn implied conscription. (A Selective Service Act was signed into law on May 18, 1917.) This conscription itself required a lengthy period for recruitment, preparation, and training. Further, since the president and secretary of war (Newton Baker) believed that American soldiers must fight as members of an independent American army, that force would be obliged to take its place on the fighting line to the right of the massive French army. The Americans would serve in Lorraine, between Verdun and, to the southeast, the Vosges Mountains. The sector had been relatively quiet for a year; it would lend itself well to General Pershing's need for ample space in which to train his troops. An American field army, Pershing believed, should eventually comprise not less than a million officers and men. For them to be distributed among the Allied divisions would inevitably mean that their contributions would be undervalued, and, where credit was given, it would be given only begrudgingly.

The First Division soon left Saint-Nazaire. The division's headquarters were established in the town of Gondrecourt, an ancient village of some two thousand set down in pastoral Lorraine. The countryside thereabouts is among the most beautiful in Europe, and in summertime, on lands the war had left untouched since the early days of the fighting, it must have communicated an ageless serenity, its pastures a velvety green, its fields, centuries in cultivation, "combed and groomed by the peasant's plow."[6] Here and there villages were fitted into the gentle valleys. At a distance, their dwellings, with roofs of dusty russet, clustered about ancient churches and narrow cobblestoned streets. All noise seemed muffled. Marshall first saw Lorraine in early summer and recorded his own impression—coolly professional in its description: "broad fertile valleys, bordered by high hills ... well-watered, not too heavily timbered for military training, devoted largely to hay and grain crops ... it appears to be healthful, is beautiful, and seems adequately adapted for training."[7]

But such a description disclosed both the idealism and naïveté of its author. He was seeing Lorraine in the flush of a rich French summer, like Crèvecoeur contemplating the ripe orchards and rich pastures of his new and raw America. Almost thirty years later, Marshall's protégé, George Patton, would take a very different view:

Lorraine was "this nasty country where it rains every day and the whole wealth of the people consists in assorted manure piles."[8] Within five months, Marshall and the First Division would subsist in a very different Lorraine from what they now—in staking out billets and encampments for the regiments and support troops—celebrated.

The soldiers would be distributed about the town and its surrounding villages and farms, to be billeted in the lofts of barns and outbuildings, usually in pairs or squads of men. Marshall and three other officers, two of them American, were assigned tiny rooms in the house of Monsieur Jouette, a soldier at the front (with his son), whose wife would become a lifelong friend. In his memoir, Marshall describes his thin spare chamber with its iron bedstead "of the Napoleonic type," and a view of a small courtyard beneath. This courtyard had a single lilac tree.

The First Division, fully formed and staffed, comprised twenty-eight thousand officers and men; in size more than twice that of the British and French divisions. Marshall's duties included finding billets and training spaces, the former especially scarce in the division's assigned area. For the most part, the soldiers were assigned in fours or fives to billets in local village barns, homes with spare rooms, or vacated buildings. They were reminded constantly that the American Expeditionary Forces would be judged by what the French saw of them, just as, there being no other division in France, Pershing and his general headquarters' staff officers would judge Sibert's division as an exemplar of American forces in training. The secretary of war did permit a relaxation of the army prohibition of drinking, but he and Pershing fretted over the possibilities of large-scale venereal infections—which amused the French. Toward the end of the war, the premier, Georges Clemenceau (a onetime correspondent who had reported on the American Civil War), suggested the establishment of houses of prostitution, the better to ensure the cleanliness of providers and clients. Pershing gave a colleague a copy of Clemenceau's proposal, suggesting he show it to the secretary of war. The latter told Pershing's colleague that if President Wilson saw the letter, he would stop the war.[9]

Training began immediately, and operations officer (G-3) training was Marshall's responsibility. The soldiers of the First Division were taken in charge by veterans of a distinguished French formation, the Forty-Seventh Division of chasseurs, an outfit of some swagger and cachet, not unlike the Big Red One of the Second World War. While their own officers drilled them in the basic rudiments of soldiering, the chasseurs introduced them to the conditions of service in the line. This involved a speedy education in "trench warfare," the operation and placement of machine guns, protection against gas, Stokes mortars, raids, field first aid, et cetera. While the full division would not be assembled until late fall (Marshall having been promoted to major in the meantime), its infantry battalions were now introduced to actual service in the trenches ten days at a time, one battalion per regiment. This continued until, at the end of a month, all had served in the line.

This phase of the training had begun on October 21, the Americans now integrated with regiments of the French Eighteenth Division in the Sommerville sector not far from Gondrecourt. Notoriously quiet—*le bon secteur*—it remained so until November 2. Then, as a result of a German raid, following a sudden bombardment, an American company was overrun, three soldiers killed, and several others wounded. Marshall accompanied the French commander, General Paul Emile Joseph Bordeaux, to regimental and battalion headquarters; eventually he interviewed company and platoon officers. Marshall was offended by Bordeaux's line of questioning of the survivors: they struck Marshall as aimed at demonstrating American passivity, perhaps even cowardice. Conscious that he was representing General Pershing, he told Bordeaux he thought the latter's queries beneath contempt, and that he intended to report them to his superior.

But Marshall had judged him too harshly; it was a misunderstanding. Bordeaux won Marshall's gratitude and admiration the next day with a moving tribute at ceremonies honoring the first Americans killed in the Great War: Corporal James Bethel Gresham and Privates Thomas F. Enright and Merle D. Hay. It evokes the sustaining tenderness of the Franco-American relationship in the Great War:

We will therefore ask that the mortal remains of these young men be left here, be left to us forever. We will inscribe upon their tombs: "Here lie the first soldiers of the famous United States Republic to fall on the soil of France, for justice and liberty." The passer-by will stop and uncover his head ... the men of heart, who will come to visit our battlefield of Lorraine, will go out of their way to come here ... Corporal Gresham, Private Enright, Private Hay, in the name of France, I thank you. God receive your souls. Farewell![10]

    .   .   .

Among the significant professional relationships in Marshall's life (including those with President Franklin D. Roosevelt, Winston Churchill, Henry Stimson, and Dwight Eisenhower), none would become more important than his relationship with John Pershing—commander of the American Expeditionary Forces, general of the armies, latterly chief of staff of the army, and after his retirement from active army service, a venerated military presence and counselor to another generation of soldiers (and, occasionally, presidents). By 1918, Pershing would be among the most famous Americans in the world, next perhaps only to President Wilson. And, like the mature George Marshall, he was very much a product of his own conscious manufacture.

Pershing's first serious engagement with Major Mar-

shall occurred on October 3, 1917, at a French training
center for American soldiers. Pershing had driven over
from Chaumont on an inspection visit, and Marshall
had laid on a demonstration for him: an American unit
would attack a defended trench. Pershing (who had been
disappointed earlier by a divisional review he thought
sloppy), watched the exercise, standing amid the divisional staff. When it ended, he turned to General Sibert
and asked him to discuss its successes and shortcomings. Sibert, intimidated by Pershing and knowing Pershing's staff had no confidence in him, gave a faltering
critique. Pershing listened to him, then to others. He
then upbraided Sibert and the divisional staff, Sibert particularly, in the timeworn manner of tough commanders.
There was silence. Pershing stared at the officers, one by
one, and turned toward his aide and driver.

At this point, all accounts agreed, Major Marshall
said something to the effect of "General Pershing, I
think somebody needs to speak up and I've been here
longest so I will." So saying, and to the shock and mor-
tification of the divisional commander and his staff, he
laid a restraining hand on Pershing's forearm.

Pershing faced him. "Go ahead," he snapped.

Now, for two or three minutes, Marshall, beside
himself with a sense of injustice of Pershing's criticism,
offered a rapid, outraged defense of the division, Sibert,
and the exercise, very much in the spirit of Lord Nelson's
defense of his naval tactics in the Napoleonic Wars: *If you
knew, my lord, what we do here, you would not write me in*

this wise. Marshall poignantly enumerated the problems, obstacles, and demands on his soldiers' energies, and the overwhelming nature of their missions and obligations. Pershing listened and moved toward his car; Marshall told him he was not finished.

"You must appreciate the troubles we have," Pershing rejoined.

"Yes, General, but we have them every day and they have to be solved before night."[11]

Tall, formidable, and stern, Pershing was not a general officer used to forthright challenges from subordinates. The effect of Marshall's outburst on those watching and listening was electric. His colleagues had watched in disbelief. Pershing, however, was one of those soldiers whose outward presentation was an unreliable index to the interior man. Like Franklin Roosevelt, whom Marshall would also challenge—always respectfully but always bluntly—Pershing was more *interested* than offended by challenges like Marshall's. The encounter, in fact, represented the beginning of the most important professional relationship, and perhaps friendship, in George Marshall's life. It would be a relationship, too, of extraordinary importance to American efforts in the wars.

The incident became famous and occupies an honored place in Marshall lore. It is regularly adduced, along with other such "outbursts," in biographical accounts of Marshall as a leader, and as a testimonial to his character. The sequel has two elements. First, that Pershing thereafter always sought Marshall's counsel on visits to the division; and, later, of course, that he saw to his promotions and his assignment, after the war, as his aide-de-camp. Second, Marshall, in his evaluation of Pershing, in the testimonials and lessons learned and descriptions of wartime leadership, always singled out Pershing's willingness to entertain vigorous and forthright criticism, provided it was (however vigorous in expression) disinterested. He never allowed it to prejudice him against the soldier who had spoken out. There was no better expression of real loyalty to commander and mission than speaking truth to power in such circumstances. A commentator much later noted that leaders of real promise and talent rarely feel themselves constrained, however junior, in speaking up—when and if they are sure of their ground. They do not do it often; their reputations for efficiency of service and loyalty to mission are well established; they honor the senior recipient of their criticism. A lesser man than Pershing, is the inference, would not have invited Marshall's confident defense of his general and his division.

But the officers who had watched the encounter were aghast. Sibert rushed to Marshall—his embarrassment can scarcely be imagined. Others assumed this would be the end of his assignment on the divisional staff. Marshall told them that the worst thing that could happen would be his assignment to one of the infantry units, to a combat billet, which was what he wanted anyway.

· · ·

Of the American generals who by force of character and accomplishment have dominated the military establishments of their day—Washington, Grant, Lee, Pershing, Marshall, MacArthur—none seems more remote than John Pershing. The nature of Pershing's genius has similarly failed to be engagingly communicated to succeeding generations. He was formidable, indomitable—"the history of America in World War I is written in Pershing's shadow because he wanted it that way."[12] His will was granitic. He held stubbornly to fixed notions of what needed to be done to win the war: the American army must be kept separate from the forces of the Allies. The native genius of the American soldier must be utilized in "open" warfare, not in static positions that neither engaged an experienced enemy nor exploited his natural aggressiveness. Though not a ruthless disciplinarian, he was ruthless in his judgments of men and their abilities, comfortable in his obligations, as he saw them, to fire commanders who did not succeed. His physical presence was intimidating, his personality, so far as men could judge, subsumed utterly in the great task before him.

Pershing had entered the military academy late—at twenty-two—from a village in rural Missouri. His cadet career at West Point was similar to Marshall's at VMI: academic mediocrity (he almost failed French), but excellence in military studies and leadership. He graduated in 1886 as class president and first captain of the corps. He retained a vivid memory of seeing Ulysses S.

Grant on the post when he was a cadet (Grant died in the summer of 1885), and he always spoke of Grant as the country's greatest soldier.

Pershing had distinguished himself for valor commanding cavalry on the Great Plains and for service in the Philippines, won a rare spot promotion at the instance of President Theodore Roosevelt (from captain to brigadier general), and later commanded the American force sent into Mexico to capture Pancho Villa—the failed mission to which Marshall had not been assigned at the end of his own second tour of duty in the archipelago. Pershing had been the most junior of the candidates seriously considered for assignment to command in France, but he had certain advantages: his father-in-law was a United States senator, Frances E. Warren, from Wyoming; he had recently had active service in the field and was known to be apt for command and physically fit; and his principal rival, Leonard Wood, an outspoken Republican close to Theodore Roosevelt, was far from a Wilsonian beau ideal as a candidate. Pershing had suffered, and surmounted, a terrible private tragedy: his wife and three of their four children had been lost in a house fire, in 1915, when Pershing was in Mexico.

Pershing was a commanding presence: erect, immaculate in turnout, wearing an expression that demanded crisp answers and efficient compliance. He was raw will. Charles Moran, Winston Churchill's physician during World War II and immediately afterward, recalled Churchill's characterization of World War I leaders as generals of "the heavy blockhead type." Like many such men—Douglas Haig, Philippe Pétain, John French, Ferdinand Foch—Pershing deployed strengths more easily subsumed under the heading "character" than intellect. But his judgments of men were acute, and though uninspired as a strategist and tactician, he was a man of steady tenacity of purpose. He was what the American Expeditionary Forces required. In important ways he resembled his own beau ideal: Ulysses S. Grant. He had Grant's imperturbability and disinterestedness, a constancy. He came to his new duties with a common prejudice: that the American soldier, volunteer or regular, National Guardsman or reserve, had a native aptitude for war; that, more than any European, he was the beneficiary of a temperament both aggressive and venturesome—and inventive.

This is not to say that Pershing was the ablest general, Lee and Washington excepted, in American history. He had nowhere near the strategic acumen of his own hero Grant, nor the organizational genius of the younger man who would become his aide at the end of the First World War: George Marshall. He also lacked the inspired and charismatic ability to lead of Marshall's contemporary (who already made Pershing uneasy, as he would Franklin Roosevelt): Douglas MacArthur. What Pershing did have, however, was an extraordinarily keen sense of talent in other men; a certain form of disinterestedness that made him interested in intelligent criticism, rather than offended by it; and unrivaled tenacity of purpose. All would be sacrificed to the achievement of the mission.

.   .   .

For Marshall and for the Allies, the period between the deaths of the first American infantrymen in November 1917 and the huge offensives, mounted by each side, in the spring of 1918, was one of painful frustration and rising danger. The American buildup in eastern France continued, regiments from several other American divisions joining the First Division in training. To the devastating Italian defeat at Caporetto in October 1917 was added the far more portentous withdrawal of almost all German forces from the east—the consequence of the Russian Revolution and the eastern armistice with Germany. In later October 1917, the Allied array comprised 176 divisions—104 of them French—against 150 German; on March 20, 1918, the Allied number had shrunk to 169, the German had risen to 192. Six American divisions were now in the country, their training mostly incomplete. Moreover, the size and quality of the Allied divisions had now deteriorated significantly (English infantry divisions deployed nine, versus twelve, battalions). The British Fifth Army, fifteen divisions, covered a front of some forty-eight miles.

There were two consequences. The first was a renewed, no-holds-barred effort by the Allies to force Pershing to "feed" American units into undersized

French and British divisions: the hated amalgamation. Pershing refused. The directive that had appointed him commander of the American Expeditionary Forces was uncompromising: "The underlying idea must be kept in view that the forces of the United States are a separate and distinct component of the combined forces, the identity of which must be preserved."[13] Feeding American battalions and regiments into training schemes that fitted them into the line, for periods of a few weeks, was one thing; placing them under French or British commanders another. Pershing insisted he would never "parcel out" American boys. In extremis he would abandon his pledge, this act the result of the German decision to undertake a campaign to win the war that spring: Operation Michael.

As operations officer of the First Division, Marshall had continued to oversee the division's training and preparations, mounting and sustaining an aggressive if static defense along its assigned sector. Marshall remembered it as a bleak and miserable time. It was, in his mind, the war's "Winter of Valley Forge." It rained ceaselessly. Training—emphasizing physical conditioning and hardening the command—and deployment in the line taxed the soldiers' endurance. Conditions of continuous cold were no help: "Many had only one pair of shoes . . . some of them did not have even one pair. When we were not cursed with mud, we were frozen with the cold."[14] Short bleak gray days yielded to long frigid nights. Marshall oversaw training in what was called "open warfare," a vague formulation of army headquarters that expressed less a considered tactical *méthode* than the commanding general's frustration with the static character of the war and the state of mind it engendered in Allied combatants. Open warfare was a factitious response to battlefield conditions that made such responses murderously foolhardy. It emphasized sudden maneuver and concentration, attacks and defenses in depth, surprise— all laudable initiatives. But battlefield domination by direct-fire weapons made their success problematic. It is interesting that the German commander, Erich Ludendorff, sought solutions to the same conditions, and these were not so different from Pershing's desires. A deadly battle sequence had long prevailed on the western front: extended artillery bombardment; an advance by long lines of infantry across a pocked and shredded no-man's-land, the advance easily broken apart by machine gunners whom the artillery bombardment did not disturb; a return to status quo less hundreds of thousands of young men. Much later in the war, in its last months, American infantry in the Argonne Forest would discover German defenses far more effective, far *worse*. They proved to be the forested equivalents of Japanese caves on Iwo Jima and Saipan.

It is not clear that Pershing believed open warfare would succeed tactically and ensure victories. The predicament it was aimed at resolving was less physical than moral. Defensive warfare as practiced in the trenches induced timid, defensive-minded frames of mind; it

sapped aggressiveness and communicable confidence
in officers. Marshall would later write that nothing was
more assuredly fatal to the needs of leadership than the
soldiers' perception that their officers were not confident,
just as nothing was more dangerous to the republic than
its congenital unwillingness to prepare in peace.

·   ·   ·

In the army patois of the time, Pershing was a remorseless *driver:* he demanded palpable results and held his
generals accountable. As late as December 1917, though
elements of three new American divisions had begun
arriving in France (the Second, Twenty-Sixth, and Forty-
Second), only the First Division was complete and completely trained. It was soon to go into the line. General
Sibert was far from Pershing's beau ideal of a crisp, vigorous, sharp divisional commander. Pershing relieved him
on December 12, sending in his stead Brigadier General
Robert Lee Bullard, his West Point contemporary, a warrior who looked like one and who promised to infuse the
division with the proper esprit.

Marshall was now acting chief of staff and a major, and
he was known to Bullard. Bullard had been sufficiently
impressed to favor him for the permanent appointment
to divisional chief of staff, but he had also learned, soon
after his arrival, that Marshall and other officers on the
staff had been outraged by Sibert's firing, and that their
criticism of Pershing's action remained both outspoken

and indiscreet. The new commander understood this and made allowances. But where another leader might have been tempted to co-opt an influential and talented critic by appointing him to an important post like that of chief of staff, Bullard saw Marshall's continuing indignation as evidence of unfitness for the assignment. He appointed another man. In so doing, possibly with intent, he taught him a lesson. Marshall admitted to an interviewer forty years later that he had been "very vitriolic" in his criticism of Pershing and his staff's severity. Marshall also noted that the officer Bullard did select was a more temperate person by nature. In his own telling, he learned his lesson and did not forget it.

It was a lesson with a price. At least one consequence was an ironic one. Marshall believed, with reason, that, had he been given the position, he would have been promoted quickly to colonel, and that this, with reasonable expectations, was almost certain to ensure a second promotion, to brigadier general. When, in fact, he was recommended for the promotion to one-star rank—by Pershing himself—it was too late. The War Department and Congress would consider no such promotions after the armistice. (Marshall would not gain promotion to general's rank until October 1, 1936.)

But this is not the irony. Had he been promoted during the war, he would likely not have been selected, on April 30, 1919, to be an aide-de-camp to John Pershing, a position he would hold longer than any other in his army career, save only his final assignment as chief of staff of the army. Marshall was Pershing's aide from May 1919 to June 1924. In effect, he was to become executive officer to the dominant military personality of his generation. His relationship with Pershing quickly followed an established pattern: the senior general, bored by ordinary administration, delegated its important duties to a willing and supremely qualified "aide." So it had been with Bell and Sibert, so it would be in his service with Pershing.

Marshall believed that he had learned his lesson. But learning lessons is very different from obeying what they enjoin. Marshall had already earned a reputation for dutifulness and reliability—a reputation that would be strengthened during the next twenty-eight years of service. He was, however, never completely able to master the effects of decisions adverse to his own settled opinions. His mastery was sufficient to ensure useful, even admirable, compliance with such decisions as his superiors might make; his friends could generally tell, though, that he "felt." Later still, Marshall would instruct his undersecretary of state, Dean Acheson, to not spare his feelings: "I have no feelings except those I reserve for Mrs. Marshall." Acheson venerated his superior, but he understood, too, that Marshall's feelings were potent and not without their influence on how he thought—and, sometimes, acted.

For his part, Bullard, an officer of fairness and equanimity, kept Marshall's indisposition in perspective: a modest and forgivable lapse in judgment colored by an admirable loyalty to a superior he believed wrong. Bullard relied on Marshall and trusted his judgment. Like Patton in World War II and Matthew Ridgway in Korea, Bullard communicated immediately and powerfully his ideal of what the division should become. Training became far more intense, discipline both more intelligent and less forgiving. The First Division remained under the continuous scrutiny of American Expeditionary Forces headquarters. It would soon be given the chance to prove itself in battle.

Marshall remained with the First Division, overseeing its training and its assignments, including a long spell in the line in the Ansauville sector. It was bitterly cold in the trenches and the billets, and the new division commander was determined to make his quiet sector an active one and to avoid the infection of defense-mindedness. Historians have long imputed truce-mindedness upon combatants fighting the West's wars; the notion of "quiet sectors," along with Christmas fraternizations, is a persistent and agreeable myth. It was not so much that the southern portions of the western front were quiet by local option as that belligerents were devoting increasingly scarce resources to "active" fronts. Bullard, before his division was called away to fierce fighting in the spring of 1918, had his division to himself, to prosecute his sector with vigor and ferocity. He managed to stir things up, by means of artillery barrages and raids. Each side took fairly heavy casualties; the Americans made good use, later, of the training their activity provided.

Marshall as planner and operations chief had a pivotal role in these activities. A Silver Star medal, awarded after the war, was a recognition of his determination, not always characteristic of staff officers, to watch and measure the consequences of divisional orders on ordinary soldiers in trenches. There would be a direct linkage between these experiences and his self-imposed duty of writing letters to bereaved families during the next war, and his insistence that casualty figures be given to President Roosevelt every week. There was a human cost to the war, and Marshall was not oblivious to it.

The designation of "staff officer" invariably communicates an invidious status in wartime. Contemporary British letters, journals, memoirs, et cetera, are full of red-tabbed officers of field grade whose lives are impossibly remote from the horror and filth of the trenches, and who, if they show themselves at all, appear momentarily in glossy boots and immaculate uniforms, are appalled by conditions on the front, and retire.

We hear much less of this among the Americans, and Marshall, like most other regulars in his cohort, chafed under the designation and its responsibilities. It was not that he was not skilled and successful in discharging them; rather, they kept him from command, and they tended to keep him away from soldiers. As divisional G-3, he used every opportunity to escape the headquarters complex and to go forward to see for himself the consequences of the orders he was obliged to prepare for Sibert, and, after December 12, for the far more aggressive Robert Bullard—for whom the notion of a "quiet sector" was unacceptable. Marshall's duties comprised the preparation and oversight of all training programs for the division and coordinating their movements in and out of the line. These movements were almost always by night to their assigned positions. We hear of him (and read in his memoir) constantly going out, often alone, in areas under direct artillery (or mortar) fire. Before the early Battle of Cantigny (May 28, 1918), he and other officers made an extended reconnaissance and returned, mainly crawling, under enemy observation and fire, to the safety of frontline trenches. For Marshall, sharing the hardships of the men was a *commitment* he understood in *moral* terms. This was one of but many traits of character that distinguished him and simultaneously offered a more real, a more human, understanding of democracy.

.   .   .

As early as March 9, 1918, American Expeditionary Forces headquarters had alerted the First Army Corps, of which General Bullard's First Division was a part, that it was sending down Major Hjalmer Erickson. The intention was that he replace Marshall as division G-3, and that Marshall join the operations staff at Chaumont. "It is believed," the order said, "that we have now arrived at the time when the General Staff here should be replenished from the troops. . . ."[15] Marshall must have been amused to see himself classified as one of the troops—if he saw the memorandum. But the memorandum stressed that the transfer was not to occur until the right time, until Erickson was ready and Marshall's services could more easily be spared. "It is anticipated that a month or six weeks must elapse before this can be done."[16]

Marshall was later ordered to the American General Staff College at Langres as a lecturer. This made Marshall a victim of a practice that had bedeviled all American divisions since their arrival—the detachment of commanders and senior staff to instruct the newly arrived. Two days after that, on March 21, the great (and expected) German offensive—Operation Michael—began. Michael's success, overwhelming in the short term, however, was not definitive. Nevertheless, it caused more than 150,000 British casualties and prompted the German commander Ludendorff to proclaim the victory "the greatest defeat in English history."[17]

Marshall was recalled from his school assignment. Pershing now offered his trained divisions to General Pétain, and the First Division took its place in the line, in Picardy, not far from the German-held village of Cantigny. In response to Pershing's order to Bullard, the division prepared itself to attack and capture the town; Marshall would devise the plans for the attack. The scale would be small but the conditions prospectively ideal for the Americans: they would have time to prepare, and prepare meticulously, for the operation. It was carried out by a reinforced regiment on May 28, and its success was, given its size, overwhelming. German casualties were heavy, the Americans held against repeated counterattacks. Pershing felt his tactic of open warfare vindicated. Marshall had been the organizer and overseer of the huge, multifaceted movement—of troops and all their vast supporting resources—that brought this array to fruition. The conception of this movement, and its execution, constitutes Marshall's outstanding achievement of the First World War, and he considered it his most useful work. Its effect was not entirely to his advantage— that is, as he saw it. Before long the word "wizard" was applied: only a man of odd, perhaps strange, gifts could carry out such an operation. The label adhered tenaciously; Marshall's reputation was now nonpareil. This was not the reputation that he wanted, though, and it was not really the reputation that he deserved. It was as though an accomplished violinist had been overheard playing a dense Chopin étude on the piano: one would remember *that* performance and the virtuosity it displayed, but would only hear others, later on, talk about the artist's accomplishments as a violinist.

Marshall's feat was the vindication, however unwanted and ironic, of Bullard's June 18 endorsement of Marshall's request that he be assigned to troop duty—that his service on staffs since February 1915 had fatigued him by "the incessant strain of office work."[18] Army patois uses "endorsement" as a neutral term meaning only acknowledgment; Bullard's was devastating: "I doubt," Bullard wrote, "that in this, whether it be teaching or practice, [Marshall] has an equal in the Army today."[19] Bullard did acknowledge that Marshall's merit should find a wider field than that of a divisional staff. Assignment to a wider field had followed, as we have seen. This had led to fields still wider—none of which, however, afforded George Marshall an opportunity to command troops in wartime. Such an opportunity, in fact, lay more than six years ahead.

Marshall took particular pride in his, and his alma mater's, contribution to the Cantigny success. He wrote General Nichols two weeks after the battle, commending VMI alumni who had distinguished themselves: "I feel sure you will be glad to know of the honorable part some of your men played in the hard fighting around Cantigny." And neither for the first nor the last time he described his own role in the achievement of a military success, with the demure qualification that "it happened to be my good fortune to have any opportunity" (of preparing the battle plans and orders for the attack). He further admonished his old friend that the information conveyed about *his* work "is for your private ear alone. It would ruin me to be making such a claim."[20]

The Marshall whom commentators extol for selflessness was not without healthy ambition or ordinary pride. Yet these were moral artifacts, as Kenneth S. Davis observed, of a less common type. Like Harry Hopkins, Marshall sought advancement "in order to 'do a job' which [he] felt he could do better than others could . . . he was endowed with what Thorstein Veblen calls the 'instinct of workmanship.'"[21]

. . .

On July 8, American Expeditionary Forces headquarters issued orders relieving Marshall from duty with the First Division and directing him to report for assignment to the AEF chief of staff at Chaumont. The accumulation of testimonials to his "special fitness for staff work," Bullard's the most influential, meant that though "my plans had all been laid to get command of a regiment in the division . . . this not only denied me that duty, but removed me from the front."[22] Marshall was assigned duty in the operations section of the American Expeditionary Forces staff—an exalted eminence to be sure, but not the eminence he wanted. Here, the currency of success was a certain kind of military intellection, patient and dogged composure, thoroughness in assembling data bearing on possible areas of attack: terrain, enemy dispositions, logistics, troops available, necessary coordination between allies.

He had left the First Division less than a week before its commitment to the most bitter fighting of the war. For fifteen months, the division had been his world. "We had been pioneers and our trails . . . had served to bind us very close to one another. . . . It was hard to preserve one's composure in saying goodbye to these men with whom I had been so intimately associated."[23] On July 12, Marshall wound up his affairs. He retired early—to be awakened by a visit from an old friend, Colonel Hamilton Smith, commanding officer of one of the regiments that had sailed with the first contingent of the division. Smith sat on the edge of Marshall's bed. The men reminisced for an hour:

> While he was talking, orders were received for the First Division to move the next day . . . this was a great surprise. Smith left immediately, and less than a week later was killed leading his regiment in the great battle of Soissons; within seventy-two hours every field officer of the infantry, excepting three colonels, had fallen. Smith and all four of the lieutenant colonels were killed.[24]

By the end of July 1918, the last of the great German offensives that had begun in March had lost its momentum, had been contained, and now, all along the Allied line, was being forced back. French and British commanders sensed that German withdrawals, however skillful their execution, now reflected an irremediable weakening: in troops' strengths, in the quality and heft of artillery support, in logistical resources, and, most important, in morale. The Second Battle of the Marne, in which American divisions made significant contributions, represented the most important Allied victory of the war to date. Paris would not be threatened again.

But at Chaumont, Marshall had been translated to a world and culture as remote from the divisional staff as the Pentagon is from an Iraqi roadside. Chaumont was a "strange atmosphere" in which quiet senior staff functionaries considered issues of "ocean tonnage, ports of debarkation, construction of docks and great depots in the SOS (Services of Supply)."[25] He reported to Pershing's chief of operations, Colonel Fox Conner, USMA class of 1898. Conner was a soldier whose reputation as an army intellectual with an internationalist perspective had commended him to the American Expeditionary Forces commander in 1917. Sophisticated, well-lettered, fluent in French, Conner was to be remembered a generation later as the man who had discovered in Dwight Eisenhower talents of unusual promise and who had taken it on himself to serve his protégé as an intellectual tutor during their service in Panama in the 1920s.

Marshall was drawn to him at once, flattered and inspired by Conner's assignment: "To gather all possible information regarding the Saint-Mihiel salient and to work on a plan for its reduction."[26] Captured by the Germans in the first months of the war, the salient—"L'Hernie"—constituted a thick bulge, perhaps two hundred miles square, into the Allied line, twenty miles southeast of Verdun. The western apex of the triangular mass was the town of Saint-Mihiel, thirty miles to its east lay the great fortress city of Metz, and between them lay important industrial facilities and rich coal and iron deposits. Almost from the beginning of the war, it had attracted General Pershing's attention as an objective suitable for operations by an independent American army: a success would vindicate his impassioned insistence that such a force, operating on its own, could gain a major strategic victory. This would, Pershing thought, show that "amalgamation" could no longer be argued by the British and French on the grounds of American naïveté and inexperience.

By July 24, Marshal Foch—appointed Allied commander in chief on April 24—had agreed that the First Army should mount the Saint-Mihiel operation "in the latter part of the summer . . . to smash the . . . salient and free the Nancy-Paris railroad."[27] The First Army headquarters would be established at Neufchâteau, and American divisions would concentrate thereabouts in preparation for the offensive. Marshall and his colleague, Colonel Walter S. Grant, began serious planning for the American offensive, adapting their plans to the divisions made available—a number that changed repeatedly. In the course of their planning, they sometimes allowed a prospective offensive only from the south face of the salient, sometimes from both the south and western "sides." Varying estimates of artillery and armor (and air) resources were provided—these too influencing the final shape of the plan that would be presented to Pershing.

"My state of mind at this period is impossible to describe," Marshall wrote. "I seemed to be getting farther and farther away from the fight, and it was particularly hard to work on a plan and then not attend to its execution."[28] There was, however, another, severer trial. Marine Major General John A. Lejeune called on Marshall one afternoon and offered him a command of the Twenty-

Third Infantry Regiment. Lejeune, commanding general of the Second (Army) Division, went to Fox Conner to ascertain Marshall's availability. Conner turned him down. On the day Marshall hoped would mark his concluding labors as a staff officer, he was ordered to Neufchâteau as an operations officer in the First Army.

· · ·

In his memoir, *Present at the Creation,* Dean Acheson remarked on George Marshall's singular ability to hold many elements in his mind, factors to be searched out and considered in their changing and mutually fructifying relationships until at last they "precipitate" a useful solution. Planning the Saint-Mihiel operation and what was to follow offered Marshall and his associate Colonel Walter Grant a rich, early opportunity to demonstrate such an aptitude. It was partly a talent cultivated at the ill-defined intersection of temperament and intellect: its elements patience, equanimity, thoroughness, and a disciplined effort; also, to consider possible enemy responses to implemented plans. Marshall confessed, forty years later, that he had "always been rather embarrassed by the fact that I submitted a number of different plans—none of them you might say conclusive."[29] It couldn't be helped: Marshall and Grant were at the mercy of changing estimates of Allied forces available in support, and of American divisions that Pershing was willing to commit to the offensive. Most difficult by far was Pershing's agreement, disappointed and reluctant, to Marshal Foch's demand for a Saint-Mihiel operation somewhat less ambitious than the First Army was preparing. (This was the consequence of early successes elsewhere.) Foch had demanded Pershing provide several divisions for service in the Aisne under a French general, and several others for an offensive contemplated in the Meuse-Argonne, also under French control. The meeting between Pershing and Foch on August 30 concluded with Pershing's obdurate refusal to consider breaking up the First Army. He told Foch that he, Foch, had no authority to break up an American force, scatter it around, and that "while our army may fight wherever you decide, it will not fight except as an independent American army."[30]

A compromise was later reached. Pershing agreed that he would undertake an immediate withdrawal from the salient once the battle had been won and that he would guarantee the First Army's readiness to undertake a second, greater offensive not later than September 25 in the Meuse-Argonne. Its aim was to be the capture of the Mézières-Sedan railhead, and, in concert with more or less simultaneous French and British offensives all along the western front, the surrender of German arms. Foch's conception was essentially that of Ulysses S. Grant in the spring of 1864: several armies attacking an overstretched enemy at *all* its vulnerable points, eliminating the possibility of reinforcing one area of operations from another's reserves.

However brilliant, this meant, of course, a logistician's nightmare: withdrawal from contact, movement to another front, the maintenance of secrecy of that movement (some sixty miles), the displacement of a force occupying the other front. This is not to mention that it was all to occur in thirteen days, and with the consequences of the first Saint-Mihiel operation unknown. Only "ten minutes consideration made it apparent," Marshall wrote in his memoir, "that to reach the new front in time to deploy for a battle on September 25th, would require many of these troops to get under way on the evening of the first day of the St. Mihiel battle. . . . This appalling proposition rather disturbed my equilibrium and I went out on the canal to walk while thinking it over."[31] Further, Marshall recalled, this

> "stand[s] out in my mind as the most trying mental ordeal experienced by me during the war . . . the harder I thought, the more confused I became, and I finally sat down beside one of the typical old French fishermen who forever line the banks of the canals. . . . In the calm of his presence I composed my mind."[32]

Marshall and Grant had worked for weeks on the reduction plan, on the positioning of the American divisions for the reduction of the salient, and all the movements and supporting operations required to sustain the coming battle. They had developed an elaborate deception plan, in which an American corps was to attack through the Belfort Gap, some 120 miles south.

The attack on the salient would easily achieve its *reduction;* Marshall's preoccupation was now, however, a "Release and Readjustment of units [during and] following" the reduction.[33] The Pershing-Foch compromise—an uncomfortable means of accommodating two fundamentally opposed conceptions ("Marshall's appalling proposition")—would become the source of the enterprise that would fix Marshall's reputation. This reputation, again, served only to promote his dissatisfaction and embarrassment, as the movement had to be managed as quickly and (seemingly) effortlessly as his dictated orders to commanders and staff in the Philippine maneuver of January–February 1914. "In less than an hour I had evolved a method for the procedure and had completed the order, which not only covered the preliminary movement of troops, but involved the regrouping of the organizations remaining on the St. Mihiel front at the close of that battle. . . ."[34]

Many hands ultimately serviced Fox Conner's initial conception of the reduction of the Saint-Mihiel salient—at headquarters, American Expeditionary Forces, and now, as finally approved and distributed to the Allied forces arrayed along its western and southern faces, in the operations section of the First Army. Marshall, now at the First Army headquarters, was assigned as an assistant to First Army Chief of Staff Hugh Drum. In this role, Marshall was charged with final coordination of the plans, with ensuring that American divisions assumed their assigned places, and, alongside Grant, with arguing for a maximum artillery preparation commencing the night before the battle. Pershing settled for a relatively brief four hours. As for divisional alignment, the First Army put its best foot forward: among the frontline attackers would be the First, Second, and Forty-Second "Rainbow" Infantry Divisions. A price would be paid later, though: there was desperately short time available between the Saint-Mihiel mission and the requirement that the First Army be on line for their attack in the Meuse-Argonne less than two weeks later. This was based on the presumption that the First Army would achieve an easy victory. Ultimately, these divisions would be the last divisions relieved at the end of the reduction. The consequence later was close to calamitous.

The battle was won in less than two days. Following a four-hour artillery preparation, at 5:00 a.m. on September 12, the attacks on the two sides of the salient began in steady rain. The First Army (seven American divisions) moved forward from the southern face. On the other side, a mix of French and American divisions proceeded. The Americans reached and overran their objectives almost immediately, and by midday on the thirteenth, the Saint-Mihiel salient was no more. Some sixteen thousand Germans had been killed or taken prisoner, at a cost of seven thousand American casualties—

far less than the expectation. Even though the German army had begun the preliminary stages of a withdrawal from the area, it was the victory toward which Pershing had strived for a year, a proving ground for American action on the grand scale.

By now, there were 1.4 million Americans in the American Expeditionary Forces. More than a half million participated in the battle, and many of the leaders of the US regiments and brigades, officers in their thirties, would become famous as commanders in the next, larger war. Douglas MacArthur, George Patton, Terry de la Mesa Allen, and Marshall were among this storied group. None, however, would taste the satisfaction of exploiting the First Army's success; they needed to move immediately on Metz. Against a ten- or eleven-day deadline, they formed part of the vast movement of forces onto the last battleground of the Great War: the Meuse-Argonne.

.   .   .   ˋ

Let us not hear of generals, Clausewitz wrote, who conquer without bloodshed. Let us not hear of staff officers, Marshall often reflected, who do not consider, and understand, the consequences for ordinary soldiers of the movements, schemes, *plans* they conceive and prepare. The battlefield (few labels are less useful in what they connote) toward which Marshall now began to organize the movement of more than a half million men was soon to become a dark arcade of slaughter. Half of this battle-field was choked in forest impermeable to sunlight, its floor a chaotic mélange of streams, marsh, ravines, and to its east, between the Argonne and the Meuse River, an operational theater all of whose advantages accrued to the defender: dominating heights carefully fortified and with clear sight lines over most of the area.

This was not Marshall's particular concern at the moment. Within ten days, he must bring into position some 600,000 men, 400,000 from the Saint-Mihiel sector. This "position" required that each division find its place in the line from which the whole attacking force would move forward at the signal given on the morning of September 26. Moreover, each division would need to secure the places for supporting artillery, ammunition, transportation, and other supply dumps; indeed, some of the artillery would begin movement to the new front even before the Saint-Mihiel operation was concluded (a total of three thousand guns and forty tons of ammunition). Marshall was also tasked with arranging for the withdrawal of 220,000 soldiers currently arrayed along the front toward which the Americans would be directed. Put crisply, Marshall "was to plan and supervise the shift of all troops out of the St. Mihiel sector to the zone of the French Second Army, then holding the line the Americans would take over."[35]

All of these activities were to be carried on at night. Trucks were available to move the majority of troops, but not *all* of them; there were but three roads, all narrow, cluttered, pocked, running south–north, to accommodate the movement. Marshall oversaw this movement after he had planned it, now working in the town hall in Souilly, from which Pétain had directed French forces during the Battle of Verdun.

Marshall's logistical prodigy earned him a new title: *wizard*. Every unit, every supporting element, arrived in its assigned location before the huge opening artillery barrage at 2:30 a.m. on September 26. He would be remembered ever afterward as a paragon of almost inhuman efficiency. He had calculated speeds, distances, load-bearing capabilities (of roads and vehicles), necessary alignments and arrays, final positions for the offensive. He had also—by tireless and unflappable oversight and liaison with dozens of exhausted, frustrated, and angry American and French officers—accomplished what Marshal Foch, for example, had considered an impossibility.

Marshall had now been made a colonel and operations chief in the First Army. Whatever gratification the achievement and its recognition may have provided was surely accompanied by a rueful reflection: this was not command—and if anything it seemed to harden a reputation of a certain eccentric *kind* of military genius. This was a reputation that, Marshall believed, would guide his future in the army; it would influence the assignments he would be given, and would, he must have imagined, deny him the highest positions in the profession to which he had committed himself. The achievement served to obscure, also, Marshall's role in the forty-seven-day campaign ahead, in the terrible autumn days of fighting against an enemy whom the terrain favored in every conceivable way. During this campaign, the bulk of the fresh American divisions leading the opening attack were woefully underexperienced: one of the American divisions, the Seventy-Ninth, charged with assisting in the capture of Montfaucon (which oversaw much of the battlefield), had never seen battle. To make matters worse, most of these soldiers had been in France less than three months; the junior officers scarcely knew the men they commanded. The Americans "had not learned the lessons the Allies had acquired at such terrible cost: against entrenched troops using machine guns and supported by artillery, frontal attacks by riflemen produce ruinous casualties and no results."[36] The left side of the advance, through the Argonne itself, was a "bleak, cruel country of white clay and rock and blasted skeletons of trees, gashed into innumerable trenches, . . . seared with rusted acres of wire, rising steeply into claw-like ridges and descending into haunted ravines. . . ."[37] The wide defile to the east, across the Meuse, lay almost entirely under the guns of the bluffs along the forest or the heights of the Meuse itself.

The great Meuse-Argonne offensive now heaved itself forward, the largest American field army ever arrayed and sent into battle. Nine divisions lined up alongside one another, six in reserve, the aggregate ranged along a front of twenty-two miles from the interior of the Argonne Forest on the west to the Meuse River to the east—the river typically seventy-five feet across and not fordable. On the western flank, the army was linked to France's Fourth Army; overlooking the Meuse was a range of low hills that provided the enemy excellent points of observation and fields of indirect fire. At 2:30 a.m., some four thousand Allied guns had opened up: doughboys, like marines in a later war, alternately wondering how anyone could survive such a barrage, dreading the enemy's ability, somehow, to do so. At 5:30 a.m., the whistles of the company commanders and Plattsburg lieutenants had signaled the line forward into a heavy fog that covered virtually all the southern portion of the battlefield. This was the beginning of an offensive—itself part of Foch's grand offensive, whose aim was nothing less than German surrender—that would claim some 26,000 American lives (of 127,000 total casualties).

Marshall believed in later years that these losses, perhaps most of them, were avoidable. In 1917, as in 1898, 1939, and still later, in 1950, the nation had been unprepared for war. The divisions that had literally begun to pour into France at a rate of 250,000 soldiers a month in the summer of 1918 were little better off than that First Expeditionary Division he had joined in Hoboken in 1917. Many soldiers *still* had not fired the weapons given them; there were reports of privates, newly joined, still without complete uniforms, and of sergeants charging five francs to demonstrate how to feed a clip of ammunition into a rifle. As for infantry tactics, marksmanship, and field navigation, some of the divisions might as well have been in their second or third week of basic training. This is not even to mention the absence of basic hardening through forced marches and long exposure to living in difficult circumstances in the field.

There was another liability: the seasoned American divisions had been the spearheads of the Saint-Mihiel offensive, and therefore were committed as *reserves* at the start of the Meuse-Argonne campaign. The two divisions in the American center, charged with the capture of the dominating terrain feature in the broad valley between the Argonne and the Meuse, were essentially raw recruits commanded by generals who themselves could call upon only the slender resources of experience in large scale operations. In terms of preparation, the Americans were far behind.

.   .   .

By the sixteenth of October, more than a million Americans were in the field, now divided among *two* field armies, the second under Marshall's old boss, Robert Bullard. Marshall was now chief of operations in the First Army (under Liggett), charged with planning further offensive operations, and coordinating the movements north by the divisions participating. However exhausted, Pershing's force now sensed their opposition was faltering, much of the enemy driven from his prepared positions, in headlong retreat.[38] A strange sequence soon followed a general order from the supreme commander (Foch), in which commanders were admonished that they need "know only the direction of attack. On this direction they advance as far as possible ... without any attempt at alignment."[39] By November 1, German lines had collapsed; by the fourth, the city of Sedan was within artillery range, and Pershing, in Foch's spirit, had ordered that a general pursuit be pressed without solicitude for flanks and boundaries.[40] Pershing went a step further. On the fifth, he sent Brigadier General Conner to First Army headquarters (Souilly) to inform Liggett and Drum that he, Pershing, wanted the First Army to "have the honor of entering Sedan."

Neither Liggett nor Drum, now a brigadier general and First Army chief of staff, was present, so Conner gave the order to Marshall, who dictated a slightly fuller version and had it transmitted immediately to Liggett's corps commanders. "We were on very intimate personal terms," Marshall wrote later, "so I laughed and said, 'Am I expected to believe that this is General Pershing's order, when I know damn well you came to this conclusion during our conversation?'" Conner did not laugh—he insisted the order be communicated at once. Marshall persuaded him to allow Drum or Liggett time to return so that they could approve it. When Drum finally arrived, he simply endorsed Conner's order (as dictated by Marshall), adding a fatal amendment: "Boundaries will not be considered binding."[41]

The consequence was chaos—ultimately, the chaos of victory, but a dangerous chaos. Pershing (and Drum) *meant* the boundary between the French Fourth Army, on the American left, and the American First Army. Those receiving the directive saw only "boundaries." A free-for-all ensued, leading to one of the bitterest contentions between American troops during the war. The American First Division simply cut across the corps to its left, in the process intermingling with the Forty-Second Infantry Division, capturing an enraged Brigadier General Douglas MacArthur in the process. Eventually, the lead First Division battalion—Theodore Roosevelt Jr. commanding—crossed in front of the Fortieth *French* Division.

All units were ordered to halt in place, and the French finally occupied Sedan—their claim to the honor beyond all argument—but not until after the armistice took hold at 11:00 a.m. on November 11. "A heroic farce," Marshall's official biographer called it, and as two of the principals, at least, chose to remember it: MacArthur and, later, Pershing, the most punctilious of commanders. Marshall was censorious: "The whole thing to my mind was out of place. The thing was, we were succeeding. We weren't there to fight each other." The long marches of exhausted troops, all at night, and most of them over terrain marked by weeks of incessant bombardment, uphill and none of it on roads, would bring the American Expeditionary Forces to the end of its soldiers' experience in the Great War. This experience would form part of the indelible memory George Marshall would bear years later as, again, he was asked to make preparations to deploy other, and much larger, American armies.

Chapter Eight

Between the Two
World Wars

With the end of the fighting came what Marshall's official biographer called the dissipation of that "moral singleness, simplicity, and intensity of purpose which is unique to war."[1] The American army, less troops selected for occupation duties, prepared to leave France. The vast majority of its soldiers prepared to leave the army.

The butcher's bill had been savage: 51,971 dead and 199,286 wounded. These were small numbers by comparison with British, French, and German—and Russian—losses, but severe all the same, painful especially in their concentration: the Meuse-Argonne offensive alone had accounted for 26,000 dead and 96,000 wounded and missing (all between September 25 and November 11, less than seven weeks). More than 3,500 American casualties occurred on the last day of the war, many sacrificed to the zeal and ambition of regimental officers determined to savage the Hun up to the last moment.

Marshall was assigned a variety of duties. For two months he served as chief of staff of an army corps (December 1918 to January 1919). In this role, he was responsible for training divisions remaining on occupation duty. Later, as a staff officer in Pershing's headquarters, he was charged with planning for a full occupation of Germany, should she fail to meet her obligations under the terms of the armistice. Finally, Marshall was assigned as a lecturer—a propagandist, really—tasked with speaking to assemblies of doughboys awaiting their port calls to return to the United States. Most were disgruntled and impatient; Marshall was to convey the big picture, to identify the causes and consequences of the Allied victory and the American contribution to it. He was also to remind the new veterans of their obligations to present a "true" picture of what their army had accomplished. How familiar such "education" must seem to those Americans of today who are aware of the military stories of the last half century (Vietnam, Afghanistan, Iraq, et cetera) goes without mention.

Among the young reserve officers Marshall had selected as assistants was a young Utah lieutenant who had been graduated and commissioned from one of the Plattsburg camps. Benjamin Caffey Jr. remained with Marshall through his service with the Eighth Corps, and after being demobilized, wrote a brief memoir of his work with him. Marshall was, Caffey wrote, "outspoken and impatient against stupidity, inefficiency, and disorder."[2] He was also, only three years after seeking General Nichols's assurance that the army did in fact hold some promise for him as a lifelong commitment, a vastly successful professional—however frustrated in his ambitions to command soldiers rather than plan for their activities and "staff" the orders of his superiors. Not long after the war ended, according to Caffey, a highly placed civilian offered Marshall a job with J. P. Morgan & Co. Caffey had found himself later at a Pilgrim Society dinner in New York seated next to Dwight Morrow, then working at J. P. Morgan, but in the waning months of the war a volunteer Red Cross representative dining in Pershing's mess in France. According to Caffey, Morrow said that Marshall had "the most brilliant mind of any man he had ever met." He offered him $30,000 a year in salary. Marshall turned him down on the spot.[3] Morrow told Caffey that Marshall was a fool to turn him down.

Marshall had preferred honorable service to riches, vocational satisfaction to the promise of wealth. There were compensating rewards: the American Distinguished Service Medal and the award of the French Légion d'honneur, at Metz, by Marshal Pétain. At the Metz ceremonies (April 1919), an inquiry was communicated by an aide of Pershing's as to whether Marshall would himself accept appointment as aide-de-camp to Pershing.

Marshall did not hesitate. The moment marked the real commencement of the most consequential relationship, and perhaps friendship, in Marshall's life: an assignment that would last for more than five years of service, rich in experiences of the kind that would enable him to view from the loftiest perspectives the issues that would preoccupy the army and nation for the next thirty years.

Well into the war that succeeded the great conflict—ended, finally, in 1918—one of President Roosevelt's advisers wondered how it was that the president had been favored, in his appointments to high posts, by so many men able to rise to the occasion presented them. In fact their "rise," and Marshall's particularly, had already begun, and whatever frustrations and disappointments lay ahead, they were prepared to master them. A new kind of school presented itself. John Pershing, soon-to-be chief of staff of the army, did not like administration. Issues that came to him in the form of questions and requests, many on matters of large national import, frequently landed on his new aide's desk. On them was a notation soon to be familiar: "Major M, take care of it."

.   .   .

The memoirs of famous generals are almost invariably of twentieth-century wars. These men were invited to set down their own recollections of what they saw and did, and perhaps learned. They are almost uniformly barren of the arresting, illuminating detail of the fighting and suffering they saw and what, if anything, it did to them. To find such testimonials and accounts, readers must look elsewhere.

George Marshall wrote no such memoirs of his generalship in the Second World War. From 1920 to 1923, however, he pieced together a memoir—the publisher's word—of his service in World War I. The manuscript has a curious history. Marshall showed it to Houghton Mifflin in 1924, which, though interested, told the author the book needed work. Marshall put it aside. Much later he asked the second Mrs. Marshall (Katherine Tupper Marshall) to destroy the manuscript, which she believed she had done. In 1940, Marshall's stepdaughter, Molly Brown Winn, found a copy in the attic of the Marshalls' home in Leesburg, Virginia. It was finally published, long after his death, in 1976.

This "memoir" is useful to any student of Marshall's life. Not because it records and deploys the useful and illuminating details of men in battle for which a reader is thirsty, but rather because of what it tells us about Marshall. As John Hay once told Mark Twain: "[Your] facts and [your] fictions will work loyally together for the protection of the reader."[4] The reader, that is, will be able to *tell* what you are like.

Here is an altogether different George Marshall, different from the somber and dutiful icon of the Second World War. Here is a young man, ambitious, often impulsive, voluble, naïve, and impressionable. Again, there is almost nothing of the suffering, of the rare exhilaration, or horror, or unendurable fatigue (and sometimes terror) of extended combat. There is similarly little by way of description of the "battlefield," itself a quaint word connoting eighteenth-century evolutions and regular volleys and formations. This is not because Marshall did not see such things. Marshall was brave, determinedly so, constantly going forward, often alone and usually on foot, often under artillery and mortar fire, often in the trenches. He was known and admired for this. It is indeed central to his character. An adolescent determination to prove himself strong and independent had matured to a dutiful determination to earn the respect of soldiers who were not working in the relative safety of staff billets. And he *wanted*, and was always denied, command "in the field." It was the high road to promotion. More than that, though, it was what a trained army officer did, or should be doing.

.   .   .

In the early 1940s, Marshall and other military colleagues formed posed, obligatory clusters around Franklin Roosevelt and Winston Churchill. Photographs that record these moments mark the conclusions of the great Allied conferences. These men evince an unvarying, weary dutifulness. Their public presentation is one of self-mastery and calm. It is hard to remember George Marshall any other way, just as it is hard to imagine George Washington as limber and athletic, as a man enjoying himself. But before the public and private personae had fully formed themselves and merged, some time in the late 1930s, we are allowed to see a Marshall altogether different from the Marshall who was chief of staff and secretary of state, from the Marshall whose *image* has become utterly, fully, establishmentarian.

The diary that forms a publisher's appendix to the *Memoirs of My Services in the World War, 1917–1918* is in part a journal of Marshall's July 1919 visit to London as an aide-de-camp to General Pershing. It discloses an astonishing, as we should say, side to him: Marshall as enthralled and exhilarated novice and commentator. The account, which originally appears in the form of letters to Lily, has a breathless quality—the writer is having the time of his life. It reveals a droll, canny element in the diarist's appreciation of those he meets and watches; it reveals Marshall's more typical human qualities.

The eight days' visit was for purposes of celebration and the bestowal of honors: decorations, testimonials, the awarding of honorary degrees (one to Pershing at Christ's College, University of Cambridge), a victory parade in London, in which a fractious mount almost ended Marshall's army career (and, in any case, broke his wrist).

The celebrants rarely retired until three or four in the morning. Each daylight hour was filled. At a palace reception Marshall noted,

> [The Queen wore] a very close-fitting gray dress with the usual small hat of gray resting on top of a high headdress ... she and the King made some colorless remark to every person. ... I walked around with Lady Curzon who is supposed to be one of the beauties of London ... she pointed out all those who occupied important positions.[5]
>
> Later, Lady Drogheda joined us. She is a very *dashing* sort of person: I left by a little private gateway in the rear of the garden and drove around to her house where she had some Scotch and talked for an hour or more.[6]

Later, at another ball, "I had the pleasure of stepping on the foot of the King of Portugal, and I think about ruined his Royal Highness."[7] At the same dance, on July 16, Marshall confided that, although most guests had left, the party became very lively around 3:30 a.m., and that he "received an intimation that [he] should ask her (Princess Victoria) for a dance—and immediately went home. General Pershing stepped on her foot and left a large black spot on her slipper. . . ."[8] Several days later, after the triumphal victory parade, at which General Pershing received a tremendous ovation, and Colonel Marshall was thrown from an unmanageable horse he had thoughtfully offered to ride, the diarist laments his having to execute a "laborious dance with Princess Mary. If she doesn't reign any better than she dances, they are in a hard way, but she is a nice sweet-looking little Dutch girl."[9]

There are still extant a few frames of film of Marshall and other officers following along in Pershing's train during his inspection tours. At thirty-eight, in a trench coat tightly belted, he appears thin, his movements quick and animated, his expressions unusually mobile—the expressions of an ardent and delighted young officer having the time of his life. He remains many years' removed from the solemnly composed military and State Department leader whom photographs record for later generations, and which will always know him this way. Marshall the American Expeditionary Forces wizard, the thrice-promoted aide to the most famous hero leader since the death of Robert E. Lee, remains an object of his own conscious manufacture and superintendence. He is as ever dutiful. But, in 1919, for the last time in his uniformed service, we sense, he is having fun.

After a tour of the principal battlefields of the late war, mainly in France, Marshall accompanied General Pershing on a brief visit to Italy—Rome, Venice, Milan. On September 1, 1919, the party sailed, on the USS *Leviathan,* for home. Huge and joyous celebrations greeted the returning soldiers: a spasm of national relief and triumph and a confident understanding that this war had ended all wars, and that the Allied victory had proved an aroused democracy and its noble allies would always defeat the armed forces of an authoritarian, militarized regime. It was an ironic echo of the delight Marshall had seen on the Champs-Élysées two years earlier— before the doughboys had proved themselves. American officers and NCOs had fretted over the raw Americans' want of smartness and discipline; French spectators had found the sight inspiriting—the rawness was ardor, idealism, the promise of the unjaded and valiant. The country had immediately imbibed the wrong lesson, just as, Marshall understood, the War Department would probably infer the wrong strategic and tactical conclusions from the army's large victories at Saint-Mihiel and the Meuse-Argonne.

His homecoming and reunion with Lily (September 8) implied neither the establishment or resumption of a life of regular hours or ease.

.   .   .

Near the end of the Second World War, Dwight Eisenhower—whose relationship to Marshall (in age and authority) bears useful comparison to Marshall's relationship to Pershing—wrote his older friend that he wished Marshall could see the fruits of his labors: the massive American armies now deployed in Europe. Their hour of triumph was at hand. It is a measure of Eisenhower's large and liberal spirit that he should credit

Marshall with the forging of the weapon that was winning the war in Europe.

This was a citizen army. The country regarded peacetime military service as the province of professionals: a small professional cohort that served in peacetime, except when mobilized enemies were demonstrably threatening. (In fact, Marshall was to take the oath as chief of staff in 1939 in a white linen suit. It would not do, it was felt, to advertise the presence of soldiers in the capital.)

The army demobilized rapidly after the Great War. By June 30, 1919, a little more than seven months after signing the armistice, more than 2.5 million enlisted men and 128,000 officers had been mustered out. By the next year, the army had shrunk to 130,000 regulars.[10] A West Point graduate, class of 1920, appeared in uniform at a hometown wedding in Ohio in 1923. An older friend asked, "Clovis, what have you done? Why is the army still holding you. . . . Can't you get out?"[11]

Pershing's rival, General Peyton March, had proposed a postwar force, a "standing army," of 500,000. As chief of staff, March had persuaded Secretary of War Newton Baker that such an army would be sufficiently large to address any likely threat to the country. It also appeared to form the cadre for the training and leading of the large levies that an external threat could, conceivably, demand. The proposal became a bill; the bill also included universal military training. In virtually all particulars, it seemed calculated to offend the sensibilities and prejudices of Congress, the country, the unions, business, and academia. Familiar castigations, echoes of earlier postwar debates about national defense, became more numerous and more strident. A large army would be Prussian, militaristic; it would be wildly expensive; it is inconceivable that, after the slaughter in Europe and Russia, any country would dare attack anyone. There was also the perdurable exaltation of Athens over Sparta: a mobilized and outraged democracy will always subdue the forces of highly militarized and authoritarian governments. As a matter of fact, the American doughboy is such a redoubtable soldier *because* he remains his own man. In this kind of democratic man, initiative, curiosity, the capacity to improvise, natural hardihood, and strength will always combine to defeat his enemy. For better or worse, this was the inclination of many.

The Senate Committee on Military Affairs listened to testimony from a variety of sources, including a brigadier general sent to represent Pershing (still in Europe). The son of a Civil War officer opposed the March plan not as a Pershing partisan but on principle. He argued eloquently, and with a daunting mastery of detail, that the American genius for war found its most useful expression in a very small regular army (say, 250,000 to 300,000 men). This, he thought, was a force sufficient to address all but the largest challenges. If much larger numbers were needed, they would form a citizen army, a national army along the lines of the American force in

France. The head of the Senate committee found this view congenial, as did most members of the committee and most of the country.

Pershing's opinions were sought. Now returned from Europe, he was a national celebrity hero, and not unlike his own hero Ulysses S. Grant, had political antennae far more sensitive than his persona—upright, stiff, formidable. He knew, too, that the March plan would never realize sufficient support to become law. Moreover, he hated March, an artillery lieutenant colonel in France when Pershing had been commander in chief of the American Expeditionary Forces. Pershing saw the chief's office as a service enterprise: *Send me what I need, promote those whose names I submit, do not presume to suggest or attempt to determine strategy.* "Temperament" does not survive very well in histories, but March appears to be a military solipsist, both unable to appreciate the consequences of his actions and words and indifferent to those consequences.

There is an anecdote that illuminates the Pershing-Marshall friendship and Pershing's view both of March and Marshall. Pershing had suggested a change in War Department procedure on a matter of small consequence—except that the procedure had been initiated by his predecessor March. Pershing asked his aide for suggestions. Marshall told his superior that he didn't like what he had read. Pershing asked him to rewrite the memorandum in a way more suitable to the purpose, as Marshall saw it. "I just don't accept this," Pershing repeated.

Finally Marshall spoke up: "Just because you hate the guts of General March you're setting yourself up to do something you know damn well is wrong."

Pershing replied: "Well, have it your way."[12]

To prepare for his appearance before Congress—on the size and character of the postwar army—Pershing and several aides came together at the Naushon Island summer home of Pershing's friend Cameron Forbes. Here, they remained for three weeks of earnest but relaxed discourse, decamping in October for the Adirondack retreat of General Fox Conner's father-in-law. Discussions were held amid the brilliant autumnal ambience of the north woods, evening entertainments (amateur theatricals included), and long walks.

The taut purposiveness and multitasking of a later day could scarcely have prepared a more compelling and convincing witness than the American Expeditionary Forces commander. Flanked by Marshall and Conner (still wearing their wartime insignia and rank), to whom he turned for facts or counsel, Pershing answered the legislators' questions and offered his own views on a military establishment appropriate to the republic at peace. In so doing, Pershing joined a discussion as old as the republic itself.

The army had already shrunk precipitously: by 1930, its enlisted strength was barely 185,000—a twelfth of that of the last months of the war. Neither the country nor its representatives were in any mood to endorse Peyton March's pleas for a regular army of a half million. To the senators' queries, Pershing returned answers that reflected Conner's and Marshall's counsel, not to mention his ebullient confidence that his army of citizen soldiers had proved a certain point. Though Pershing may have harbored misgivings about his force's martial potential—in 1917—these had long since vanished: "The fact is," he said, "that our officers and men are far and away superior to the tired Europeans."[13] They had won the climactic campaign of the war, and had proved that a large force of regulars need not be maintained in time of peace.

Congress had already heard Conner's testimony, and Pershing was familiar with his arguments: there should be a small regular army for emergency deployment; universal military training could prepare a citizen army, much larger, if circumstances warranted. "If American citizen armies," he had written, "extemporized after the outbreak of war, could do as well as Washington's Continentals and as well as the citizen armies of Grant and Lee, what might they not do if organized and trained in time of peace?"[14] Like later advocates of universal military training and conscription, Conner rooted his positions in the fertile soil of *civic* obligation broadly and equitably shared: the argument of Athenian democracy and of most—but not all—of the founders.

The National Defense Act of June 4, 1920, authorized a regular force of 280,000 soldiers, backed by a strengthened National Guard and an organized reserve; the Guard and the reserves to be responsible for preparing citizen soldiers, and maintaining their readiness for mobilization should the president, Congress approving, believe an emergency demanded more than regular forces. The organized reserves would comprise, among other elements, ROTC units on university campuses and the citizens' military training camps, lineal descendants of Plattsburg. A few reserve officers were appointed to the general staff. Universal military training was not approved: it was fated to be a good idea in the minds of several generations, but no more than that—a good idea.

Among the singular ironies of American history, universal service has always attracted the most attention in times—immediate postwar periods—when the political will for its implementation has been weakest.

·   ·   ·

After the Great War ended, and before the next fateful global conflict would begin, Marshall watered his roots at his alma mater. He declined again to be considered as a superintendent at VMI—it is certain he would have been the prime candidate had there been a "search"—but the incumbent, Brigadier General William H. Cocke, and members of the board were sympathetic to his reasons for remaining on active service. This was not least due to their pride in the reputation Marshall had earned in the army. He also responded, in a remarkable letter dated November 5, 1920, to a request from an older friend, Brigadier General John S. Mallory (USMA class of 1879), a language instructor at VMI. What lessons had Marshall derived from his service in the war, Mallory asked. Marshall's response was singular:

> To be a successful leader in war four things are essential, assuming you possess good common sense, have studied your profession and are physically strong.
>
> When conditions are difficult, the command is depressed and everyone seems critical and pessimistic, you must be especially cheerful and optimistic.
>
> When evening comes and all are exhausted, hungry and possibly dispirited, particularly in unfavorable weather at the end of a march or in battle, you must put aside any thought of personal fatigue and display marked energy in looking after the comfort of your organization, inspecting your lines and preparing for tomorrow.
>
> Make a point of extreme loyalty, in thought and deed, to your chiefs personally; and in your efforts to carry out their plans or policies, the less you approve the more energy you must direct to their accomplishment.
>
> The more alarming and disquieting the reports received or the conditions viewed in battle, the

more determined must be your attitude. Never ask for the relief of your unit and never hesitate to attack.[15]

Marshall was able to persuade John Pershing to deliver the commencement address at VMI that June. By now a thoroughly practiced distinguished visitor, Pershing performed admirably. He spoke in Jackson Memorial Hall, congratulated the graduates, and visited Lee Chapel at neighboring Washington and Lee University, along with the grave of Stonewall Jackson in Lexington. These pilgrimages got him into trouble with a few Northern scolds; Pershing made Marshall draft soothing letters to them for his signature.

Wounds of a war fifty-five years in the past still festered here and there. Earlier, Pershing and Marshall had stopped to survey the Shenandoah battlefield at New Market, where the VMI cadet corps had participated in a successful charge against an enemy force under the hapless General Franz Sigel. Marshall inquired of a local farmer, a man in his eighties, where the charge had begun. He added, "I have General Pershing with me. He was commander of all American forces in France."

The man did not respond.

"I said," Marshall repeated, "that is General Pershing over there. He led our armies in France."

The man spat. "I heard you the first time," he said.

It would be too much to say that Marshall, on these

unending travels, almost all by train, played Boswell to Pershing's Johnson. But Pershing was invigorated by travel: their traveling accommodations—drawing rooms, et cetera—were commodious, and Pershing, ramrod stiff, pressed and buffed on duty, lapsed into holiday mode on the road. Marshall called him "boyish." Pershing was exuberant, funny, not incapable of mischief; his trust in Marshall was, of course, complete. He could unbend. One night, traveling from Boston to Washington, the two men sat up late drinking Scotch, the gift of a friend of Pershing's. The general decided it would be good fun to carry a glass through the train (it was after midnight) to one of the sleeping cars, knock on a compartment door, awaken US senator George H. Moses, and offer him the drink. They had the wrong berth. A young woman's voice, unamused, told them they had the wrong person. According to Marshall, Pershing (in his shirt-sleeves) ran through the cars to get back to their drawing room, laughing uncontrollably, terrified they had been caught. The next morning at breakfast, the senator, by now informed by the young woman what had transpired, gave them a hard time.

Pershing was very stern on duty, and the amusements and badinage of his relationship with Marshall on the road stopped dead when they returned to the office. The duties to which they were called seemed to so require the ascetism of popular memory.

Pershing was appointed chief of staff to succeed Peyton March on July 1, 1921. His tenure as chief, lasting until September 13, 1924, was unremarkable: a continuing struggle to maintain some semblance of an effective regular army in a time of fiscal parsimony. Marshall's duties as an aide now assumed a character familiar to his duties as aide, assistant, deputy to other general officers. Like Liggett and Bell (and like the astute and prescient observer Fox Conner), Pershing had learned that he could repose special trust and confidence in Marshall—not in the formulaic mode, in which the aide would assist Pershing in what he was doing, but substantively. Pershing was bored by the routine of office and its heavy burden of reading, study, and resolving small matters. Increasingly staff memoranda came out of his office with the solitary notation: "Major M." The meaning was simple: *Take care of this and tell me what you have done, in my name, later. I don't really want to be bothered.*

Marshall took Pershing at his (implicit) word, using his chief's long absences to impose his judgments on matters sometimes beyond his pay grade. (Pershing was gone from the office sometimes for as long as four months.) Marshall dismissed a delegation of Tennessee Republicans, for example, who had come to see General Pershing to urge him to seek the Republican nomination for president. He sensed, correctly, that Pershing would be a terrible naïf in national politics, not unlike, in significant ways, his hero U. S. Grant. Nor did he hesitate to confront the general, always respectfully, but always tenaciously, on matters in which the general seemed to

allow emotion to overrun judgment. Pershing yielded—
usually with sheepish grace: "Well, have it your way." He
continued to accompany Pershing on long railroad trips
around the country, as he had done in the year between
the dissolution of American Expeditionary Forces headquarters and Pershing's appointment as chief of staff.

Both before and after Pershing's elevation to chief,
Marshall wrote thoughtful appreciations of the American experience in the war, one for the G-3 (operations
section) of the First Army's report, another for the
Infantry Journal. In this latter venue, Marshall argued,
at a time in which such views were unusual, that the
American tactical experience in the great Argonne campaign should be admired and remembered only for what
it was, not as a useful adumbration of campaigns and
battles in the next war:

> It is not intended . . . to belittle our efforts in the
> latter part of the war, for what we actually accom-
> plished was a military miracle, but we must not
> forget that its conception was based on a knowl-
> edge of the approaching deterioration of the
> German army, and its lessons must be studied
> accordingly. *We remain without modern experience
> in the first phases of a war. . . .* [16]

And Marshall added that there was the irrefutable
lesson that "the unprepared nation is helpless in a great
war unless it can depend upon other nations to shield it

while it prepares. . . . More than a year elapsed after our declaration of war before we were able to undertake an offensive action."[17]

The consequence of Marshall's service with Pershing was an extraordinary appreciation of issues that would challenge and dominate his professional life after 1939. Commentators remark on Marshall's (and Eisenhower's and Omar Bradley's, among others) unusual growth in the early years of the Second World War. Most of this growing, in Marshall's case, had actually happened before 1925. With two unusual assignments immediately ahead—in China and as assistant commandant of the infantry school at Fort Benning—his preparation for the most significant challenge of his life, as yet unimagined and unimaginable, would be complete.

Chapter Nine

China

L ike those of the ablest members of his cohort, Marshall's assignments and duties were almost always profoundly satisfying in substance and in the range and variability of the challenges presented. Command of soldiers is rewarding to long-service professionals. "Command," however, is an outworn word, not unlike "battlefield" or "garrison." It denotes absolute authority, as it must sometimes be. But, more commonly, it requires the full retinue of the skills of leadership. Young American soldiers are American citizens first, products of a culture that has habituated them to resent being "told what to do." They must be *led*, not commanded. Many successful officers have themselves been former enlisted soldiers; they appreciate this dynamic. Like schoolteachers, they find satisfaction in the progress and improvement of their performance of work. "Command" has always been the desideratum of an officer's career, of his sense of what he should be doing; for most it is what they want to do. Whether exercised at battalion or divisional level, its satisfactions are of a piece.

Most of Marshall's contemporaries, like Marshall himself, did not regularly command soldiers. The array of available assignments in the twenties and thirties was broad, but it comprised few opportunities to command battalions and regiments, the units requiring field-grade commanders. Other duties were multiform: service on staffs, military attachés, duties as exchange officers, specialists of every stamp. Fortuitously, Marshall had tours of duty among soldiers—blessed intervals of command in circumstances that brought him close to his men and their families, service that was not only earnestly dutiful but also fun (a jarring word to apply to Marshall's sources of professional satisfaction). He would command infantry battalions and regiments—and, at the end of the thirties, a brigade: in China, Georgia, South Carolina, and Washington State during those years. He found his soldiers, and the younger men in the Civilian Conservation Corps for whom the army was given early responsibility, representative of young American males of their generation. For the most part bright, these were coachable, engaging men, responsive to sympathetic rather than authoritarian leadership. They had enlisted for many reasons, most of them not ignoble. It was the sharp remoteness of their lives that tended to endow them, in the public mind, with the qualities that the cliché of "command" sustains.

The nation celebrates the character, talent, and versatility of American soldiers who rose to the highest commands during the Second World War. Theirs was a generation commissioned between 1900 and 1920. For all these men, at least half their preparation for the challenges of the early 1940s came between the end of the First World War and the outbreak of its successor on September 1, 1939. For the army, these were years of niggardly budgets, continuous reductions in strength, meager pay (which was actually cut in the early 1930s). This was added to other, subtler reductions in compensation, diminished prestige, reductions in rank (immediately after the end of the Great War), and desperately slow, begrudged promotion. Albert Wedemeyer, USMA class of 1919, would spend fifteen years as a first lieutenant. Omar Bradley and Dwight Eisenhower, members of the famous West Point class of 1915, were *majors* in the army; theirs was a class, incidentally, whose net attrition by 1940—when they returned to the academy for their twenty-fifth reunion—was but 15 percent.

The wonder (shared by many) is that such officers, men of parts and prospects, remained on active service during the long period between the wars. There can be no question of capabilities: most had already been demonstrated, others would soon be displayed on the largest stage imaginable. Many of these officers were paragons of selfless dutifulness and the most profound patriotism, no doubt. But there are other explanations for their continuing service; explanations, that is, other than unself-regarding allegiance to code and creed. One of the

dangers in explaining their abiding love for service is to
be found in the easy sin of presentism, of considering
their service according to the cultural expectations of a
different age, a time that both stimulates and rewards
certain forms of ambition, particularly for early *recognition* ("He was the youngest man ever to have . . ."). This
is not to mention our culture's obsession with celebrity,
with meretricious display of the appurtenances wealth
has made possible. We must be wary of imputing the
confused (and confusing) values of today with those of
the military professionals of the 1930s.

One argument that has been advanced to explain
their continued active service, as hardy as it is inaccurate,
is that these officers were men of independent means and
assured social standing. Supposedly, like their English
military contemporaries, they were like the imagined
narratives of many so-called historians, wellborn and
with "outside incomes." This was not true: few officers
had such fortunes, and the most notorious of those who
did would have served had he no money at all. George
Patton is demonstrative.

Other explanations are more useful. These apply with
particular aptness to the George Marshall of 1919 to 1939.
Among these is the fact that military rank, *grade,* as a
signification of stature and standing in the officer hierar-
chy, counted for relatively little. In the army of, say, 1930
(Marshall was then a lieutenant colonel and assistant
commandant of the infantry school at Fort Benning),
soldiers of significant accomplishment and promise were

known and judged far less by their peacetime rank on a lineal list than by known, demonstrated capability and accomplishment. These aptitudes were particularly associated with their achievements in the war in France. This service was by far the most consequential of Marshall's career to date. Whether he was a lieutenant colonel or "full" colonel meant very little, other than several hundred dollars in annual salary. At Fort Leavenworth (as a lieutenant), he had been instructing senior captains like Hunter Liggett and John McAuley Palmer. Marshall's standing in the estimation of such men did not vary with his rank. As for money, field-grade officers were not well compensated in dollars, their cash emolument was but a component of a comfortable "package" of benefits. Among these benefits were lovely and commodious quarters, duties in posts overseas that conferred benefits that few, if any, American could afford at home. Sergeants in the Fifteenth Infantry in China routinely employed four household servants. Most army officers considered themselves fairly well-off in comparison with civilians.

There was an ordered spaciousness to the lives of these men (and all, still, were men) and their families. Marshall had enormous responsibilities as Pershing's senior aide, responsibilities to be exercised in a rich variety of venues and assignments, and among a variety of political and business leaders of the country. He and his contemporaries seemed to lead professional lives less cluttered, less jammed with corroding interruptions of a superficial character, less fragmented by continuous reassignments and movements. Not only this, but they had a more ample leisure. Just as the Latin root *licere*, "to be free," suggests, these men exercised freedom in travel, in extensive reading, long furloughs away from the army, and in the pursuit of serious avocations. When they did move, they moved in comfort, and their lives overseas were *comfortable* and unhurried. Modern presidents and senators, in media profile, are always said to scan eight or nine newspapers daily to absorb incredible amounts of data and knowledge each morning. Senior officers of Marshall's interwar generation, in contrast, wrote one another long letters. Invariably, these letters attest to the cultivation of avocations, to long periods of exercise (undertaken for joy, not for meeting self-imposed "workout" regimens).

Eric Larrabee remembers the rather hardscrabble lives of career NCOs and officers on remote army posts: disregarded assignments amid isolated, straitened circumstances. Soldiers lived a dusty integrity in a culture hospitable to the development of character and characters. This was a time in which there were many roads to eminences scarcely imaginable to professional soldiers hoping to retire, with luck, as colonels. In their cohort were hundreds of officers who *studied* their profession, who read deeply and widely in history, who developed and sustained the capacity to greet what was new with fascination, not with loathing or fear. The George Marshall who would lead the army would have little interest in hiring and promoting officers just like himself: he wanted soldiers who could do, brilliantly, the things that need to be done. Whether they had perfect cookie-cutter careers, error-free and orderly, meant less than their capacity to grow. In 1940, the first two officers he promoted to the grade of brigadier general were Joseph Stilwell and Terry de la Mesa Allen—each a man of acerbic, offbeat personality, each with a checkered record, each with enormous promise.

.   .   .

China was an unusual and somewhat exotic posting. When the Marshalls arrived in China on September 7, 1924, the country was a violent, fragmented state. The feeble Manchu dynasty had been overthrown more than a decade earlier; Dr. Sun Yat-sen's successor regime, proclaimed a "republic," proved no less capable of establishing an authoritative regime than the last Manchu. And, though Americans had withheld military forces from the international constabulary guarding Western concessions in Tientsin after the Boxer Rebellion, they now committed a reinforced regiment. This was the unit to which Lieutenant Colonel Marshall—who had sought the assignment—now reported. It happened that the commanding officer, newly appointed, was not expected until November. Marshall, denied that coveted privilege in the Great War, was now an acting regimental commander. His mission was simple enough: protection of American citizens and, in the slippery diplomatic usage, interests in the bustling commercial city and its environs.

The Fifteenth Infantry had a certain éclat. It was a swank not unlike a detachment of the French Foreign Legion. The average age of its soldiers was in the late thirties—these were long-service professionals whose crisp discipline and gleaming appearance were proverbial. These were the type of military professionals that our culture might still recognize, the type that does not walk around in peacetime covered in medals and ribbons for cable news but rather serves and executes as the needs of the nation demand.

There were incessant drills and long periods of indoctrination, not excluding the required mastery of rudimentary Mandarin. There were restrictions on movement until senior NCOs were certain they could trust newly assigned soldiers to behave when they went out into the city. They did not always behave, of course; drunkenness and VD rates were among the highest in the army, and much of Marshall's energies were devoted to finding, and implementing, ways of bringing such things under control.

The regiment comprised one thousand soldiers— an absurdly understrength force given the prospective dangers. The regiment's units were on continuous alert, testing its leaders' resourcefulness. This was due to the chaotic political atmosphere, dominated by warlords and their own "armies," at least one of them numbering more than 100,000, fighting intermittently and battening off local peasants' produce and livestock. Another of the armies, badly defeated by a temporary alliance of the other two, passed through and around Tientsin in retreat: 100,000 soldiers confronting scattered outposts of a half dozen American infantry, typically an NCO and several privates. These NCOs were directed to offer the Chinese soldiers food and tea in exchange for the soldiers' handing over their weapons. Through discipline and a kind of Kiplingesque sangfroid, the Americans succeeded with no "enemy" casualties. Marshall was credited with much of the success: "I snaffled a nice letter of commendation out of the affair which is worth my three years in China," he later wrote to a colleague at home.

Marshall had a large house near the American compound, maintained by a staff of five. Marshall, Lily, and Lily's mother, Mrs. Coles, lived a comfortable routine. Lily wrote to a friend that her tour in China was a three-year shopping spree. Marshall—who had taught himself Mandarin to a level of proficiency that allowed him, as an officer of the military court, to interrogate witnesses—continued the physical regimen established at Fort Meyer. There were long early-morning rides around the glacis of the American area of responsibility, two hours of squash tennis in the later afternoons, and summertime encampments at Nan Ta Su, where companies of the Fifteenth were sent for recreation and training in the field.

Again like characters in Anthony Powell's *Dance to the*

Music of Time, certain army officers had now begun to drift into Marshall's successive worlds of service. That is, to drift, disappear, and then, five or ten years later, in different ranks and appointments, appear again. The officer corps of the mid-twenties, indeed the officer corps down to the beginning of World War II, remained tiny: promotions came at a glacial pace (when they came at all); the criteria of stature and approval were in the officer brotherhood's knowledge of who you were, what you had done, who your patrons were, what jobs you had held. Three vivid characters now appeared in Marshall's professional ambit: Edwin Forrest Harding, Joseph J. Stilwell, and Matthew B. Ridgway. They were all assigned during his tour with the Fifteenth Infantry. Harding was an army literary man, poet, and wit and a Fort Benning protégé of Marshall's. Stilwell was a near contemporary of Marshall's who, with MacArthur and Patton, would later form a triumvirate of brilliantly gifted army characters. And Ridgway, like Stilwell, would also serve with Marshall in the forthcoming assignment at Fort Benning.

Marshall's official biographer recorded the impressions of a lieutenant visiting Nan Ta Su (the Fifteenth's summer retreat), observing Marshall, who had been reverted to regimental executive officer, Colonel W. K. Naylor having arrived the preceding winter to take command. To the lieutenant, Marshall's duties seemed pathetically infra dig. He had known Marshall by reputation as the G-3 of the First Army, the familiar of Hunter

Liggett and Fox Conner, and Pershing's effectual deputy (even if assigned as "aide"). Now, the lieutenant wrote, "I began to wonder what the army had for me, [when] ten years after a great war ... one of its large figures was busily engaged in teaching little groups of eight men how to handle themselves in the field."

However observant this lieutenant, he seems to have missed an important feature of the Marshall persona. That is, that Marshall took the same incredible pleasure in teaching and leading—and training—a few score soldiers. This was not unlike the pleasure Marshall took in serving as chief of operations for the whole First Army. Baffled students of the interwar army, stunned that such men would undertake duties so obviously beneath their talents and educated capabilities, misconstrue the nature of the vocational professions. One historian glibly notes that Marshall languished "in a series of ... dead-end assignments."[1] The historian might as well have written that a brilliant Oxford don, spending a morning conducting tutorials with three or four undergraduates, was wasting his genius; he could have been spending his time writing an important book or lecturing five hundred students. Marshall was, however, learning and relearning the lesson basic to the judgments of all senior officers: the lesson that Wellington repeated to his friend J. Wilson Croker two days before Waterloo. Croker had asked the duke how he thought the Allies would do when they engaged, as all knew they would, Napoleon's army. Wellington pointed at a British private, standing across the street alone. "It all depends on him, doesn't it?"

.   .   .

The senior American officer in China during the period was Brigadier General William Connor, an astute judge of the American, and foreign, predicament. The presence of such military detachments was both tolerated and resented. The forces assigned to watch over the concessions and nationals would be powerless to defend their charges in the face of concerted offenses against them. Connor recommended either a much more substantial American presence—more naval and marine than army—or American withdrawal altogether. So long as civil war—into which the current uncoordinated campaigns of the tuchuns (provincial warlords) had plunged the country—continued, the American presence was precarious, and virtually useless.

Like Stilwell, Marshall would later become identified with failed American initiatives in China. His three-year residence and tutorial in Chinese politics and culture left no useful influence on his service in 1946, when he would be asked to undertake what is now considered a fool's mission: brokering a truce between Mao Zedong and Chiang Kai-shek, and using the truce to engender serious negotiations between the two sides that could lead to a permanent truce between nationalists and communists. In 1925 he had confided to Pershing that "how the Powers should deal with China is a question almost impossible to answer."[2]

Not long before the Marshalls left China in May 1927, George Marshall replied to a letter from Brigadier General William H. Cocke, superintendent of VMI and successor to General Nichols. Cocke's letter solicited Marshall's interest in succeeding Cocke. He declined, and with the rigorous self-scrutiny he shared with few, said that he would never "throw up my army career for the uncertainties of your job, unless financially independent." His other reasons, linked, are more interesting: "My ideas and methods would too probably arouse the restricting hand of a board of visitors. . . . This may seem a strange point of view for one accustomed to the restrictions of army life. But it has been my good fortune to have had a number of jobs where I could pursue a pretty independent course. . . ."[3]

It was, of course, true. Like many of the army officers who would come to the highest grades and responsibilities during the Second World War, Marshall had either made or been given opportunities that both stretched and nourished his talents. Such was his reputation, and such were his friends and superior officers, that his work was *assumed* to be useful to the army.

.   .   .

In China, Marshall had been, briefly, paterfamilias of his regiment—serving as acting regimental commander at each end of his assignment. It was a role he cherished. Now, in the spring of 1927, he was assigned as a professor at the Army War College. This was an institution bearing Mr. Root's legacy, which, as late as 1927, still fulfilled dual purposes: as a planning adjunct to the general staff and a nursery for field-grade officers thought to have special gifts as planners, but also as a school with an advanced curriculum in military strategy, history, and tactics. Marshall was expected to lecture several times a week. He and Lily were given a handsome columned house on the grounds of the college. Within three months, an event, perhaps long dreaded but never seriously contemplated, would redirect his career, and that of a generation of American soldiers whom he would now touch in direct and profound ways.

Despite the admirable housing arrangements the Marshalls enjoyed at the Army War College, a cloud hung over the couple: Lily had begun to fail late during the Marshalls' residence in Tientsin, and their leisurely voyage home, so far from aiding in recuperation, had only seemed to make her condition worse. That condition, almost certainly congestive heart failure aggravated by a diseased and swollen thyroid, persuaded her doctors that an operation was required. If successful, the operation could be definitive, restoring her to health, to a condition that, if sustained with care, could ensure recovery. Performed at Walter Reed on August 22, the operation proved to be far more complicated than the surgeons expected. Lily's recovery was prolonged and terribly painful. "A heart is a very slow thing to heal," she had written to John Pershing, "but I pray that I may be back in my own house at the War College before so very long. And I will look forward to seeing you."[4]

Lily's death, from heart failure, came unexpectedly on September 15, 1927. The definitive testimony to the character of Marshall's marriage is of course his own, in words that recall Ford Madox Ford's "this is the saddest story I have ever heard." They appear in a letter to John Pershing, who had written his protégé on the occasion of Lily's death, not long after the Marshalls' return from China. "My heart goes out to you very fully," Pershing wrote. Marshall, reading the letter, thinks at once of Pershing's almost unimaginable loss and terrible bereavement in 1915, when he lost his family to a house fire. *I have been through this: there can be no worse.* And it is the quality, the character of Lily and Marshall's marriage, that makes its ending so desolating. His life and labors in the army apart, Lily was everything else.

All of Marshall's friends rallied around, Pershing among them, determined that he find and be given work that would absorb him utterly. On October 14, 1927, Marshall had confessed to Pershing that he "could do better" if there was a campaign or if he had cultivated a club life previously. Nevertheless, Marshall remarked that he would "find a way."

Army Chief of Staff Brehon B. Somervell understood that a pressing duty demanding a concentrated effort was the best antidote. He offered Marshall a choice of three new assignments, one of which proved to be a lifeline: assistant commandant, the infantry school, Fort Benning, Georgia. Marshall arrived there on November 10, 1927, with his sister, Marie Singer, who would look after him. The following morning, he began work, initiating the single most influential period of military education at an army school in American military history. By experience, training, temperament, and intellectual predisposition, Marshall was suited perfectly to the position of assistant commandant. And, as it would turn out, the nation would be ever in debt for this providential suitability.

Chapter Ten

Teacher

Sometime during his tour in China, Marshall, observing a company-size tactical exercise, had come upon a lieutenant laboring over a written order. The field order prescribed his soldiers' mission and the various coordinating instructions he thought required by the situation. Marshall later told friends that he knew the officer, that he was bright and promising (having finished at the head of his class at the infantry school at Fort Benning), and that he, Marshall, was aghast at the young man's inability to communicate the essence of what needed to be done to his seventy soldiers.

This lieutenant had been taught the formulaic rigmarole of the time, he believed he must adhere to it, and he was trying to fit his situation to the standard multi-paragraphed field order. It was as though a novelist had been instructed to write in rhymed iambic pentameter. Right then and there, Marshall decided, "I wanted to get my hands on Benning." Two or three years later, he did, as assistant commandant of the post. Marshall's title was misleading. In effect, he was made an academic dean with complete control over curriculum, faculty hiring and firing, and pedagogy. The commandant—a general officer who was an old friend—was the college president. This old friend ran the post, its administration, and the soldiers assigned duty there. Marshall's appointment represented a convergence of inspired personal rehabilitation and serendipitous professional opportunity. He needed absorbing work. The army—halfway in time between the end of the war in France and the final acceleration of events that would lead the United States into the successor war—was the rich beneficiary of the appointment.

The interwar period was a time of fertile military imagining about the next war. Its philosophers and theorists included Billy Mitchell, J.F.C. Fuller, Liddell Hart, Giulio Douhet, and Heinz Guderian. The Benning Revolution, as Marshall's time there (October 1927 to June 1932) was soon known, was much less a revolution in theory than a revolution in intellectual and professional culture and *attitude*. Douglas Southall Freeman saw in Robert E. Lee "the imagination of an engineer"; the characterization suits the Marshall of the infantry school.[1] What tactics are likely to work? How can young officers be educated and trained—and *habituated*—to make rapid tactical judgments and decisions in circumstances of confusion and stress? "Benning" was for company-grade officers: their business was not grand strategy but leadership of infantry companies or battalions of citizen volunteers or draftees (almost all of whom, in combat, were terrified). Those enrolled in the courses comprised lieutenants, in the company officers' course, about 150 strong; and captains and majors, in smaller numbers, in the advanced course. There were also various refresher courses and short programs for National Guard officers.

In his first year, Marshall attracted and hired as able a military faculty as the country has ever known— including Omar Bradley, Joseph Stilwell, and Forrest Harding as department chairmen. He left them alone. Bradley remembered visits from Lieutenant Colonel Marshall only two or three times in three years. Marshall embodied a principle: find and hire the best, and let them go about their business. Some two hundred future generals, faculty included, served at the infantry school when Marshall was assistant commandant. Marshall knew or had watched most, not excluding exchange officers from the marines like Lewis Burwell "Chesty" Puller and swashbucklers of little academic aptitude like Terry de la Mesa Allen. He judged them neither by their grades or class standing, but by his assessment of how well they would do leading soldiers in war. There was no "black book"—Marshall never kept one. (Like his English contemporary Bernard Montgomery, he had a famously wicked memory, sometimes too wicked.)[2]

Marshall formed his judgments in other ways. He spent much time slipping into lectures, classes, and demonstrations—watching and listening, and listening particularly for tactical solutions to assigned questions that were unusual, innovative, and that hidebound regulars, friendly or enemy, would rarely consider. On one occasion at least, after hearing an instructor contradict a student officer and reject his solution, Marshall stepped in and praised the student for trying something that had not been tried before.

Marshall was a student of successful teaching. An officer instructor who read a prepared lecture from behind a podium did more harm than good, he believed. He ordered all prepared lectures discontinued—in favor of prepared talks. These were to be engaging (if ordered ruminations) by the teachers. They were allowed to use note cards. They were instructed also that, if their business was done before the allotted fifty-five-minute period was fully used, they were to let the section go. They were to teach tactics by means of useful examples of the kind likely to recur in any theater, in any country. Demonstrations were routine, as were field exercises led by advance course students commanding elements of the 3,500-man Twenty-Ninth Infantry Division assigned to Benning for that purpose. The demesne was ninety-seven thousand acres (of which the "post" represented less than 2 percent), so the terrain was suited ideally to maneuvers. Marshall insisted that they be mounted in remote parts of the area. He insisted that "umpires" conducting the battles continuously introduce unexpected changes in enemy deployments, friendly forces, and matériel. Above all, he stressed the elements of chance, obscurity, danger—the things that inflected the battlefields of the future, as they had the dank arcade of the Argonne Forest.

Marshall had prepared what is now recognized as a classic of military exposition: the principles and challenges that war has always presented can be learned if taught intelligently. *Infantry in Battle,* undertaken by soldiers working for Marshall (though published two years after his departure from Benning), presents a variety of small-unit engagements, all drawn from Allied and German experiences in the Great War. Each has a map and a brief narrative of how the engagement was fought. The most eloquent—and accurate—summation of Marshall's understanding of how combat leaders should be prepared for the next war appears on the first page of *Infantry in Battle,* a primer for leading smaller units in a variety of tactical situations. Whether the statement was written by Marshall or by the editor of *Infantry in Battle,* Captain Forrest Harding, is uncertain. What is plain, however, is that it is an accurate summation of Marshall's conviction:

> The art of war has no traffic with rules, for the infinitely varied circumstances and conditions of combat never produce exactly the same situation twice. . . . It follows, then, the leader who would become a competent tactician must first close his mind to the alluring formulae that well-meaning people offer in the name of victory. To master his difficult art he must learn to cut to the heart of a situation. . . . [3]

This mordant observation recalls Ulysses S. Grant's canny remark about Union generals early in the Civil War. They were always thinking of Napoleon or Frederick the Great. "Unfortunately for them, the rebels were always thinking of something else."[4]

Marshall understood how to introduce change to a settled culture, a culture famously resistant to reform and change: *Suaviter in modo, fortiter in re.* It was a matter of earning assent from faculty and administration and cultivating understanding among student officers. Marshall at Benning taught and led by who he *was,* but also by an extraordinary acuity about the nature of wars and combats that would populate the futures of lieutenants and captains. He moved quietly around the post, usually alone, dropping in on classes and demonstrations, joining officers for meals and—perhaps less welcome to the academic community—insisting on wide participation in the sort of after-hours socializing especially obnoxious to people who need, simply, surcease. He put on pageants, animated a large fox hunt, insisted on athletic competitions. He was, literally, flinging himself into his work, his escape from bereavement. Photos of him are among the last such pictures of a tense, coiled, *thin* George Marshall; there is visible no effort at a smile for the camera.

It is evident that Marshall's own mentor twenty years earlier, John F. Morrison, had laid a permanent foundation for the American army's thoughtful consideration of what elements of war—infantry war—endure, and which are transient. Marshall had learned from a master teacher, and he had watched other officers in France. (He later claimed he had studied the leaders of twenty-seven of twenty-nine divisions in battle in France.) He believed that he knew what had made them successful: the retention of the capacity to make judgments in situations of terrible stress that were accurate, useful, and could be translated rapidly into simple but successful action.

By a cruel serendipity, Marshall had found himself in a situation ideally suited to his needs and talents. He made the most of his opportunity.

.   .   .

Lily had died in September 1927. Sometime in the late spring of 1929, Marshall met a widow visiting from Baltimore, the houseguest of friends in nearby Columbus. Two years younger than Marshall, Katherine Tupper Brown had lost her husband a year earlier to a deranged gunman and a former legal client of Mr. Brown's. She was tall and handsome, rather soigné, an alumna of Hollins University in Virginia and, briefly, a stage actress in Britain and the United States (much against the will of her father—he was a Baptist minister). The Browns had three children: Molly, seventeen; Clifton, fifteen; Allen, thirteen.

Marshall fell in love, mounted an efficient and successful campaign to win Mrs. Brown's hand, and they were married in Baltimore on October 15, 1930. The marriage was a successful partnership, enormously happy and not, as we shall see, without its own, and singular, tragedy later on. John Pershing served as best man at their wedding.

The Marshalls returned to Benning almost immediately, and Katherine was plunged into a world as strange to her as any she had encountered. Army social culture in 1930 was starchy. It was filled with rituals, quirky usages of precedence, ceremonials, unignorable social expectations. Katherine mastered them immediately, it seemed, and became, by all testimonials, a classic army wife: an ideal complement to the senior officer and (in effect) commander of the infantry school. She was a woman of grace, composure, good sense, and good spirit. It was, for both, a love match. Theirs was a marriage tender, zealously private, cherished all the more for the tragedies each had endured. To the children he was "Colonel Marshall," and with them and Katherine he seemed to have experienced the real delights of settled family life for the first time in his life. Again, it was the most unfortunate of circumstances that had led him to this point, but, as many can attest, the opportunity for love rarely presents itself amid perfectly tender pastures.

Chapter Eleven

Fort Screven and
Vancouver Barracks

The lieutenant in China who had thought Marshall's talents wasted in "teaching little groups of eight men how to handle themselves in the field" might have been better served by watching Marshall in his new posting: Fort Screven, Georgia. Here, he might better have understood the sources of his man's satisfactions. Trained and famously fitted for one kind of duty (the kind his China-era observer recognized), Marshall preferred another. The new post, where the Marshalls arrived in June 1932, was of ancient lineage, situated on the northern end of Tybee Island, some twenty miles south of Savannah. Here, Marshall was assigned command of a battalion of the Eighth Infantry Regiment (whose headquarters, with two other battalions, was at Fort Moultrie, near Charleston). He was also post commander.

George Marshall was now staff officer nonpareil in the American Expeditionary Forces, dean of the army infantry school, a temporary colonel at thirty-seven, and in command of a shrunken battalion of four hundred at a remote post in Georgia. In this new role, Marshall would exchange conventional courtesies with local politicians and ensure that the post's foliage was trimmed properly. "He personally saw to the laying out of vegetable gardens and chicken yards and had the troop messes prepare extra portions of food and put them up in containers for sale at cost to men with families."[1]

For all its perceived lack of classical military dazzle, Fort Screven captivated Marshall. It was perhaps the gentlest venue Marshall was ever to live in, and, in 1932, congenial to his needs and dispositions. He was always comfortable as paterfamilias, as head teacher and counselor to young officers and enlisted soldiers whose trials he not only understood but also keenly *felt*. The army of 1932 was at its interwar nadir: 120,846 soldiers, its budget virtually without provision for equipment, armaments, or research. It was absorbing pay cuts already enacted, to which mandatory, monthlong *unpaid* furloughs had just been added. And, as a final indignity, the army had to accept that raises for promotion had been eliminated.

The battalion's training requirements were not onerous, but Marshall was a devoted counselor, supervisor, and presence in his soldiers' lives (and those of their families). He saw almost immediately that an initiative by the new federal administration could be both the army's resuscitation and salvation. It touched Fort

Screven from the beginning: President Franklin Roosevelt asked Congress to approve a bill establishing the Civilian Conservation Corps (CCC) in March 1933 that would enroll a quarter million jobless young men. They would be assigned to work camps all over the country, with the mission of performing "useful public work ... forestry, the prevention of soil erosion, flood control, and other projects."[2] Within four months, some fifteen hundred camps had been established, organized in districts around the country, and were already receiving their full complement of CCC initiates.

The only institution capable of administering such an ambitious program was the army. In its servicing of the president's initiative, it spared itself from further threatened cuts in its size and budget, and more than this, it served a corollary civic function. The men who the CCC employed furnished large numbers to the army several years later when it began, slowly, to grow. And, for the NCOs and younger officers who worked directly with the young men, the CCC was a school of leadership of the kind citizen soldiers would require. An officer wrote Marshall that "this work is onerous and probably distasteful to the Army as it is not exactly military work but I feel that it is the salvation of the Army ... the Army is the only governmental agency ... able to handle this proposition."[3]

By the end of spring 1933, there were two CCC camps at Fort Screven, each run by soldiers and officers from the post. The army's CMTC (Citizens' Military Training Corps) summer camp was handed over to reserve officers that the army had to summon to active duty—another unlooked-for benefit of the program. By September, Marshall, now promoted to colonel (the rank he had worn by brevet fifteen years ago) was assigned to Fort Moultrie, South Carolina, as Eighth Infantry commander. Consequently, he assumed command of a CCC district of nineteen camps, some seven thousand men.

Life and labor at Fort Screven and nearby Fort Moultrie "keeps me away from office work and high theory," Marshall once wrote Pershing. He and Katherine had been warned: "You will never like Savannah. The people there do not know the Army people at Screven. Savannah is a closed corporation, sufficient unto itself."[4] But the Marshalls loved Screven; as they would do in all subsequent postings, they sought the *ton* of the nearby city (here, as elsewhere, beginning with the Episcopal church), made friends of them, and in the process, cultivated their new friends' interest in the post and its people. The army of the thirties was remote; too many of its officers seemed strange, even exotic cranks, none of them from families anyone *knew*. But the Marshalls—Katherine a game and interested partner in the effort—transcended any such caricature. Marshall left virtually every assignment in the 1930s, in the United States, with strong, useful relationships among local governors, senators, mayors. The most prominent among them would be Senator Jimmie Byrnes of South Carolina (which proved useful later on); Governor Charles H. Martin of Oregon;

and Charles G. Dawes of Chicago, Pershing's logistics eminence grise and former vice president of the United States.

Their lives at Fort Screven were both immunized against the most painful depredations of the Depression (Katherine's inherited income helped), and softened by the perquisites of command on a quiet, traditional army post. Theirs was a huge house at the end of the invariable officers' row, the structure sited to ensure its veranda caught the soughing summertime Atlantic breezes. All the houses reflected a "certain mottled dignity . . . and were surrounded in season by blossoming oleander and bright orange wildflower." There were beaches, tennis courts, and available "strikers"—enlisted soldiers who for a few dollars "did" for the Marshalls whatever wanted doing. Here and at Moultrie, also, Marshall began to know Katherine's children, and know them well, especially during their long visits from schools. This life and its satisfactions were invigorating and reassuring. This life, however, was now to be exchanged for an assignment the least welcome and most unexpected of any in Marshall's army career.

.　　.　　.

In a letter dated October 3, 1933, the adjutant general of the army—James F. McKinley—wrote Marshall that he was shortly to be assigned as senior instructor to the Illinois National Guard and as chief of staff of the Thirty-

Third Division, in Chicago. Anticipating Marshall's disappointment, McKinley added that Douglas MacArthur, then in his third year as chief of staff, had told the requesting authorities in Chicago that Colonel Marshall was the best of infantry colonels and that the assignment offered emoluments connected with the position.

The Marshalls left Charleston on October 20, 1933.

This was a shock, and an unwelcome one. He had been at Moultrie only a few months, and to be deprived of regimental command in order to serve as an adviser, and staff officer, and with a National Guard division, seemed on its face singularly unfair. The appointment was the consequence of an odd circumstance. The divisional commander, a lawyer in civilian life, had asked for an old friend from World War I days. The chief of staff denied the request—the officer being ineligible for the assignment. MacArthur promised the commander, Roy Keehn, an appropriate substitute, and Marshall was selected. Just before the adjutant general notified Marshall of the new assignment, Keehn had happened to see an old friend—Charles G. Dawes, the former Supply Corps general in the war and vice president of the United States. He was now a banker, but he had remained close to Pershing, and he had known Marshall casually, but well enough both to have sensed his métier and learned something of his career.

When Dawes heard of Marshall's appointment, he was outraged: "What? He can't do that! Hell no! Not George Marshall. He's too big a man for this job. In fact, he's the best goddamned officer in the United States Army!"[5] Keehn's response is not recorded, but Marshall, if not outraged, was terribly disappointed. He wrote MacArthur himself, asking that the chief of staff reconsider. MacArthur refused, but the evidence arguing malice—MacArthur trying to punish Marshall, Pershing's protégé—is weak and entirely circumstantial. Moreover, MacArthur told Keehn, according to the adjutant general, Marshall was an officer of outstanding ability. MacArthur also told Keehn, a few months later, that he had in mind making Marshall chief of infantry, a two-star billet (Marshall having been promoted to full colonel only in September 1933).

Marshall's admirers, it was said, were shocked. They regarded the assignment as a dead end.

.   .   .

A sometime colleague at Benning, Major Truman Smith, was army attaché in Berlin during much of Marshall's tour of duty in Chicago. They corresponded, and the following excerpts—one from a letter Smith sent Marshall in January 1936, the other from a talk Marshall gave an assembly of Chicago businessmen in 1935—present a striking juxtaposition:

Smith to Marshall:
The German military expansion is the greatest which the world has ever seen in time of peace.

The most powerful if not the largest army and air force in Europe is coming into existence under a strict wall of secrecy. . . . Germany is either going to expand in Eastern Europe or the western nations are going to have to stop it.[6]

Marshall on the State of the Army (speech to Chicago businessmen, 1935):

The Thirty-Third Division here in Illinois has one tank company—in Maywood—a company of unusually high morale and training. It has not a single tank, it may get one lone tank before the year is out—its complement is twenty. . . . Our rifle is a thirty-two-year-old model. Can you picture a 1903 model of an automobile, an airplane or a radio . . . ?[7]

The Marshalls found Chicago bleak and cold, the city plunged into depression. The Thirty-Third Division, ten thousand strong, functioning gamely but with no sense of urgency, seemed not much better off. The division was averse to innovation, given to unexamined routine, its part-time soldiers using the equipment and wearing the uniforms of a war now seventeen years in the past. About half the soldiers were Chicagoans; they met one night a week in local armories and attended encampments for two weeks in the summer. A predecessor of Marshall's noted that the National Guard had been "content with close order drill, limited firing practice, 'spit and polish,' and near 100% attendance at Armory inspections and Summer Camps." It was understood that assigned officers of the regular army had to advise tactfully because, however idle the National Guard's activities seemed to be, their troops would respond sullenly.

Marshall confessed in letters to friends that he missed his duties in Georgia and South Carolina. However, his new duties engaged an aptitude under long and careful cultivation, and which, as much as any, constitutes the heart of his preparation for wartime. This might be called an instinctive evangelism on the army's behalf, but an evangelism that understood, by instinct and experience, how to engage young American men in military pursuits. Regardless of the austere and formidable Marshallian *affect,* part-time soldiers—reservists, draftees, guardsmen—were drawn to him. They sensed in him a certain humanity and understanding; they saw an impatience with militaristic rigmarole, paperwork, activity that did not serve the mission. "It seemed to me that my main function was to protect the troops against my staff," he wrote a friend.[8]

"Drills" were to be executed with military efficiency, no more, no less. But what was most important was the organization of tactical exercises that would test soldiers and their officers in the field—in encampments, but crucially, in command post exercises: war games without troops. (This, as Forrest Pogue remarked, at the same time Hitler was preparing to invade the Rhineland and Mussolini Ethiopia.) Later, there were more elaborate maneuvers in which tanks and artillery batteries were marked with stakes. And, finally, in 1936, his last summer with the Chicago Guard, there were division-size maneuvers in Wisconsin comprising more than twenty-five thousand men. In this latter case, Marshall himself commanded an "enemy" brigade with a promising infantry major assigned as his operations officer: Matthew B. Ridgway, whom Marshall had known and watched in China and at Fort Benning. A certain comedic pathos distinguished these maneuvers. An ancient reconnaissance plane was ordered to provide surveillance and intelligence, but its pilot had no experience. On one occasion, the pilot communicated that he could see enemy trucks pulling wheelbarrows when, in fact, they were towed artillery pieces.

Marshall argued the army's cause among Chicago's business and political elite, often introduced by his old friend, former vice president and now Chicago banker Charles Dawes, or by the division commander Major General Roy Keehn—an attorney who represented the Hearst interests in the city. He spoke at luncheons and dinners and civic club meetings, usually about the army's needs and mission, but also increasingly about the darkening international situation that could one day require the army's participation.

This was the time, more than at any other in his army career, that Marshall's frustrations and ambitions were exposed, always at discretion, usually in letters to close friends, Pershing included, but also in notes to much younger officers like Charles Lanham and Edwin Forrest Harding, both of whom he had known at Benning, both to become general officers later on. To Lanham, he confided that an able officer "of low rank has a hard battle to fight, particularly with himself; keep on working hard; sooner or later the opportunity will present itself." Harding had been editor of *Infantry in Battle* and was known as a brilliant young officer. To him, Marshall was more blunt: "I am awfully tired of seeing mediocrity placed in key positions, with brilliancy and talent damned by lack of rank to obscurity. There are so many junior officers of tremendous ability whose qualities the service is losing all advantage of. . . ."[9]

He was remembering his own service as a young officer, but he was no longer young. Marshall would turn fifty-six on the last day of 1936. If he was to attain a position in the army to which he knew his service and capabilities surely entitled him, Marshall would have to be promoted to general officer rank by 1936. The mandatory retirement age was sixty-four. He would not, that is, be eligible for the very highest positions, and rank (including the position of chief of staff) after December 31, 1939.[10]

To a later age in which achievements and promotions are both the evidence and addictive reward of success, it seems almost incredible that an officer of Marshall's attainments and reputation should not have been promoted to brigadier general fully seventeen years after his distinguished—and famous—service in World

War I. We know, we can sense, Marshall's anguish. It did not affect the nature or quality of his service, it did not corrode his judgment. He was not embittered. But it did demand he speak up in his own behalf to his most trusted mentor. He wrote Pershing.

"I am determined not to exert political influence in my effort to be recognized, and I do not want to follow the usual course of writing to a number of senior officers soliciting letters from them," Marhsall noted. What he wanted, he told Pershing, was simply to have the secretary of war *look* at his efficiency reports and recommendations. "I am prepared to gamble on my written record in the War Department before, during, and since the war, for I have been told that no one else in the list of colonels can match mine," he wrote on November 19, 1934. He added that his *assistant,* as G-3 at the First Army, had long since been promoted a major general—in 1929! (Marshall, held to service as a "brilliant staff officer," however exalted in his colleagues' estimation, was not promoted by the end of the war because he had not commanded a regiment or brigade in the field.) And, though Pershing had recommended him for promotion to brigadier, that recommendation, like others, was tabled in the War Department with the end of the war and the precipitous demobilization of most of the army. By the end of June 1920, Marshall was returned to his permanent rank: major. Had his labors earned him this?

Again, Marshall was to be disappointed. It was not until May 1936 that he learned, definitively, that he was on the list of new brigadiers to be announced in September. Pershing wrote the good news but added that Marshall's name would go forward as junior to several others on the list who had simply had more time in grade. The sclerotic army promotion system, operating at a time of military penury, still worked by seniority. Marshall was promoted on August 26, 1936 (effective October 1), and on October 1, received orders to brigade command: Vancouver Barracks, Washington, Fifth Brigade, Third Division. He wrote an old friend that, "should a situation develop where I could have your services, nothing would please me more, because you are very much the type who does things in spite of hell or high water."[11]

That old friend was Lieutenant Colonel George S. Patton.

.   .   .

Ordered to command at Fort Vancouver with collateral duties in supervision of CCC outposts and camps in the Northwest, Marshall, with Katherine, made his farewells to Chicago. They drove cross-country and arrived at their new home in October 1936. Years later, Marshall, recounting different assignments and duties, was—for so coolly rational a judge of his own labors—given to strong superlatives: "the hardest duty I ever had," "the most important contribution *I* ever made." Brigade command and life as post paterfamilias at Vancouver Barracks must surely have qualified as his most pleasurable. And it was pleasure made bittersweet fairly early, by a warning from Chief of Staff (and old friend) Malin Craig that he would not leave Marshall at Vancouver for long. As it turned out, Craig and his deputy chief of staff were preparing a way forward in Marshall's career: in the War Department, in another Washington.

Marshall's official biographer called his service at Vancouver a kind of "physical and spiritual conditioning" for what lay ahead: his final duty with troops and the last army assignment that both demanded and permitted he spend long periods in the field. Like his army contemporaries, he watched the weltering international crises of the late thirties with a sense of the country's probable involvement in the conflicts they pointed toward. He corresponded with army friends in Europe and Washington who reported on Hitler's rearmament program, the growth of the German air force, his reoccupation of the Rhineland, and on the army staff's labors to persuade the federal administration to increase army budgets and size.

Soon after his arrival in Washington (State), Marshall quietly addressed a medical problem that had first troubled him in Chicago—an irregular heartbeat. The cause was similar to that which had aggravated Lily's heart condition: a malfunctioning thyroid. An operation was performed in San Francisco. It was a success, and its effects soon noticed. Marshall was no longer a man in a hurry: he grew heavier—slightly, not unattractively so. To this point in his army career, he had fought an intermittent campaign against a compulsion to work too hard too long; he recognized in himself what a later age would call stress-related symptoms. Even his efforts to mitigate their effects had a faintly manic charge: workouts of one kind or another morning and night; ceaseless recreational activities like those he imposed on the community at the infantry school—amateur theatricals, charades, hunts. He had always been an officer of taut nervous energy, unable to put his work behind him, and, until the mid-thirties, a regular smoker. Photographs of Marshall in China once depicted an officer almost scrawny, posing uncomfortably in arranged tableaux.

.   .   .

The satisfying round of duties—post paterfamilias, brigade commander, visible military representative to citizens and civic leaders in Portland and Vancouver, planner of maneuvers, constant visitor of CCC camps—was interrupted late in June 1937 by an incident that excited national attention. Three Soviet pilots, having taken off from Moscow for a flight over the North Pole (destination Oakland, California), suddenly set down on the post airstrip, just short of their Northern California goal. Marshall took charge, dealt with excited newspaper and radio journalists, and arranged, with the governor of Oregon and mayor of Portland, a parade through the city, a celebratory lunch, presentations to the pilots. The episode brought Marshall a minor celebrity in the Northwest.

Most satisfying, on grounds personal as well as professional, was supervision of the CCC camps in the Northwest. There were twenty-seven, virtually all of them unusual assemblies of young men in their late teens and early twenties with extensive geographic, ethnic, and vocational diversity. Nearly all of their assigned labors were what another age would call environmental. This time, though, was education for useful citizenship. And—though the campers could not have known it at the time—this experience was useful for service in the armed forces three or four years hence. For Marshall, it was also further education in democratic leadership: the CCC men were not soldiers, but they might become citizen soldiers. Leading them required education, persuasion, and explanation more than the simple issuance of orders. This was the kind of leadership successful generals would provide in the Second World War.

This work moreover provided Katherine Marshall, who often joined her husband on trips to the camps, the opportunity to join him on overnights in the woods. Sometimes, they could even fish the streams of the Cascades for dinner—just as, more than thirty years earlier in the Oklahoma Territory, Marshall had brought down morning quail for breakfast.

Perhaps Marshall sensed that his tour of duty at Fort Vancouver—virtually an idyll by his standards and expectations—would be the last assignment in his army career that provided a measure of settled pleasure, a retinue of fulfilling duties, and a happy period of service.

Contemporary accounts describe him as serene, particularly well suited to the role of post paterfamilias, and fully restored to abundant health both by the satisfactions of his work and the final elimination of his inability to cease work when there was no work to be done. Four years later, writing an old school friend, he noted ruefully that he'd had sixteen days off between the end of his tour of duty at Vancouver and the date of his letter.

Toward the end of Marshall's tour of duty at Fort Vancouver—May 11–13, 1938—he visited Fort Missoula (home of the Fifth Brigade's sister unit). Both, with other regular forces and National Guard regiments, were soon to carry out an annual duty: field maneuvers. Marshall commanded one force. He proposed, ordered, and executed an unorthodox nighttime attack, which, though his staff feared it would displease his superiors, delighted the umpires—one of whom, a divisional staff officer, was Mark Clark, then a major. Clark would later hold high command in the Far East during the Korean War; Marshall would remember him.

.　　　.　　　.

Army politics are sedulously masked. Superiors and contemporaries had always expected George Marshall would be brought in from the long round of assignments away from Washington, DC, and the War Department. He had left Washington Barracks two months after Lily's death in 1927; he served successively at Fort Benning, Fort Screven, Fort Moultrie, and now in Washington State. Sought or unsought, these postings had provided a rare education in, precisely, those things whose mastery would qualify Marshall for the peculiar range and nature of duties soon to devolve on him. More than any officer of his generation, he understood both the character of his democracy's relationship to its army and—more important—the character and culture of the young men whom the country would soon call, in millions, to military service. Like Omar Bradley and Dwight Eisenhower, he would be cherished as well as admired for this quality: as a general who understood the aspirations and needs, and quality, of his citizen soldiers; who would know what he was asking of them, and who would, his own protestations to the contrary, *feel* their anguish, exhaustion, fear, and pain. Whether his superiors in Washington fully understood the métier of the brigadier general they now ordered to army headquarters cannot be known. But Army Chief of Staff Malin Craig was a staunch ally and admirer.

In February 1938 John Pershing was reported to be desperately ill. Marshall was now alerted to take charge of the arrangements necessary for his funeral. Pershing rallied—as he would soon rally to his protégé's service. On July 6, 1938, Marshall, among the most junior brigadier generals in the army, took up his duties on the general staff as chief of war plans.

Chapter Twelve

Conclusion: A Soldier
for Democracy

Along with Alfred P. Sloan, president and chairman of the board of General Motors, Peter Drucker, theorist and lifelong student of the science and art of management, extolled Marshall as an exemplar of its most successful practices. He was, in short, an austere prince of the Industrial Age. Like Sloan, Marshall was responsible for the transformation and extraordinary growth of his organization. How he effected that transformation and oversaw that growth, and how the American army fulfilled the purposes for which he was preparing it, constitutes an unexampled testimony to Marshall's leadership.

But this was management—leadership—of a singular kind. Like Drucker, Winston Churchill praised Marshall's managerial skills. At war's end, he called him the organizer of victory. He had not led the mighty armies his country sent forth to the battlegrounds of the greatest war in history. He had *built* them. It is a heartfelt tribute, very far in spirit from the condescension that tinctured Churchill's own army chief's—Field Marshal Alan Brooke's—appreciation of Marshall's achievement. Brooke had been quick to point out that Marshall's experience in war had been limited, remote from battle. As much might have been said of the experience, up to World War II, of Dwight Eisenhower, Omar Bradley, and Matthew Ridgway. But Churchill had watched as Marshall organized and prepared his army, as he directed the formation of its many and varied components, and as he redesigned its principal maneuver element—the division. Churchill had also watched as Marshall selected and monitored the work of his nation's leaders; in fact, he had devised and supported the legislation that enabled him to appoint gifted younger leaders to high positions that the earlier purblind processes of "seniority" would have denied them. Churchill had watched as Marshall integrated the labors of the army with those of sister services and, most important, with those of the Allies. Marshall was the principal agent in the fulfillment of Fox Conner's prophecy: the next time the American army fought, it would be as a member of a powerful coalition. Churchill admired equally Marshall's service as principal military counselor to the president and the president's administration. This is also not to mention Marshall's effectiveness as the army's spokesman and advocate before everyday Americans, business leaders, and members of Congress.

Marshall prepared and built this army. His qualities of mind, temperament, and character, in fusion, proved perfectly apt for the purpose. Contemporary commentators and latter-day historians have striven laboriously to define other elements of that character that surely includes dutifulness, selflessness, self-discipline, and a palpable sense of honor. Like his seventeenth- and eighteenth-century Virginian forebearers, and like George Washington, he had trained himself to live according to a creed that he would follow all his life. "It valued self governance, discipline, virtue, reason and restraint."[1]

David Hackett Fischer uses the phrase "moral stamina" in defining the core of Washington's character.[2] It might accurately be applied to George Marshall, too. Marshall's accomplishment bears comparison, in a human enterprise as remote from the management of people as it is possible to be, with a great finished work of sculpture in marble. That is to say, its distinction is very much the consequence of its having been wrought in a medium singularly difficult and unforgiving. So, if the familiar American label of distinction "CEO" is to be applied to Marshall, its usual connotations demand significant amendment, as do those of simple "management." Drucker saw in Sloan and Marshall trained qualities of disinterestedness, utter devotion to the mission of the whole without calculation of benefit or debit to the leader. Drucker also saw aloofness, ruthlessness, discernment in delegation. Such things explain much of the success of their organizations' work. For example, since neither Sloan nor Marshall could manage all the components of his organization, each must have found, hired, promoted—and fired, when necessary—those best suited to the function each component demanded.

In looking for these leaders, Marshall was interested fundamentally in whether they could do well the thing required—whatever their other duties that had no link to what they were asked to do *now*.[3] Marshall was not looking for great men; he was looking for the *right men*. Marshall based promotions and assignments of leaders on their ability to achieve missions assigned, and to attend to the welfare of their soldiers. It was not ruthless to remove a leader from command if he failed in such duties. It would be an exercise of moral weakness and poor professional judgment *not* to relieve such leaders. To fire an old friend, or to fail to promote an old colleague who did not measure up—these were simply the commonsense requirements of the job.

Marshall was a CEO encumbered by a thick variety of requirements to explain and to justify certain actions, decisions, and plans—not to a sole (and compliant) board, but to many superiors. Moreover, until Pearl Harbor, he was working to prepare a growing organization for "work" as yet unknown, and on behalf of citizens who often opposed the use of that organization in the work for which it was being trained.

Soon enough, Marshall would become a grand strategist, a role for which his English friend Field Marshal Sir John Dill thought him less well prepared than for his other responsibilities. But, again, Marshall would be a strategist whose understanding of his nation's defense requirements had to be adjusted continuously to those of his supporters, and, after December 7, to those of allies. To build and prepare an army was one thing; to determine where, and how, and for what ends it was to be employed was something else again.

.   .   .

To achieve the tall task set for the United States in World War II, Marshall relied on what might aptly be described as the pedagogy of experience. At every point in his life, beginning in his boyhood, Marshall seems to have encountered peers, superiors, and experiences that shaped him into the man that the nation would rely on to defeat enemies of democracy abroad. From his involvement in the Great War to his administration of CCC programs, Marshall not only developed the logistical capabilities that would be central to the United States' victory in World War II, but he also learned how to understand (and thus, motivate) the everyday men and women who would be responsible for effectuating the grand strategy he and others developed behind closed doors.

The near providential set of experiences and relationships that shaped Marshall were especially important
to his leadership in this second great war because the
army over which Marshall assumed effective command
in midsummer 1939 was a shriveled, pathetic thing. It was
palpable testimony to the settled ascendancy of indiffer-
ence and hope over common sense. The army comprised
174,000 soldiers and 14,000 officers (in size, among the
world's armies, it ranked with Bulgaria's and Portugal's).
Furthermore, it represented, in numbers of troops, just
over 2 percent of the country's adult male population.
The army's units, detachments, headquarters, some 130
in all, were distributed around the country, many occupying "forts" whose raisons d'être were nothing more
than that they had always been in their present loca-
tions. There was no deployable division. (There were in
fact five divisions, "little sketchy things," but only two
comprised major combat elements.)[4]

In 1933, Marshall, then a lieutenant colonel, had
commanded a battalion at Fort Screven. A battalion,
Marshall told a colleague, was—virtually the world
around—a tactical maneuver element of eight hundred
men. Marshall's, however, had two hundred. Remark-
ably, most American battalions were of the same size six
years later. Their soldiers carried 1903 Springfield rifles
from the last war, and their only anti-tank weapon was
the .50-caliber machine gun. In 1939, the whole army
could field only twelve American-built tanks. Soldiers
training in the field still wore the familiar kettle-shaped

helmet of the Great War, and in colder parts of the country, when training in the field, puttees—the doughboy's calf-covering against the cold of the trenches in France. Private soldiers were paid $21 a month. Horse cavalry still trained on large posts in Texas.

The course of the army's transformation from a tiny force of less than 175,000 soldiers in 1939 to that of an army of 8.3 million in 1945 represents a prodigy of improvisation, planning, and public advocacy. The army's development and growth, somewhat but not wholly synchronous with the escalating dangers and threats to the country (down to late 1941), as they were perceived, faced many obstacles. For as desperately as the army needed funds, soldiers, and armaments, neither the president nor Congress was prepared to authorize such things in ways that seemed responsive to rational requests carefully rooted in argument and data. President Franklin Roosevelt responded to the army's entreaties in frustratingly unpredictable ways—as did the congressional committees before which Marshall made his case. Roosevelt, "equipped with numberless sensitive antennae which communicated the smallest oscillations of the outer world in all its unstable variety," never allowed himself to get very far ahead of the country, or where he thought the country "was."[5] Especially frustrating was to be his determination to arm *Britain* at the expense, so Marshall came to believe, of the needs of the *American* army.

Here, of course, the president was anxious to demonstrate to the American people that the country's role was going to be one of supply, support, counsel, and encouragement, in return for which Britain's military and naval successes would serve to keep German arms away from the United States and her interests in the western hemisphere. The United States would be the Arsenal of Democracy. Roosevelt was far more sanguine about Britain's survivability in 1940 than Marshall and most army opinion. He was certain that his decision to respond to desperate British pleas for weaponry—almost anything the country could spare—would be vindicated in Britain's desperate labors to defend itself and, eventually, to defeat Germany. Congress was soon to insist, however, that General Marshall as chief of staff of the army and Admiral Harold Stark as chief of naval operations certify that any weaponry or matériel sent to Britain was truly surplus: unnecessary to the defense of the United States.

The Marshall-Roosevelt relationship, like that of an arranged marriage that works out, would grow to a solid partnership based on mounting respect and mutual confidence. This was a partnership, though, without the felicitous grace notes of warmth and delight that characterized the president's friendship with the prime minister or with friends like Harry Hopkins or General Edwin "Pa" Watson. For its part, the American people subsisted in a perfect state of cognitive dissonance: dreading what seemed likely to come to them, but hoping that it would not come, and therefore refusing to acknowledge that preparations for that response to its coming were truly necessary. It was strange, especially given the fact that, by the spring of 1940, Americans sensed that the German triumphs in Europe would one day threaten the United States and draw their country into war.

The army needed soldiers. It needed leaders at all levels. It needed money, and it needed both to prepare and train itself for every military eventuality. It needed to persuade the president and the American people that to ignore or to refuse to respond to these imperatives was irresponsible, perhaps calamitously so. Whatever Marshall's achievements as a manager or CEO were to be, they were achievements wrought against desperately complicated, possibly intractable, difficulties.

.   .   .

Over the next seven years (beginning with the July 29, 1940, issue), Marshall appeared on *TIME* magazine covers six times, usually in stylized, head-and-shoulders depictions that bear the stamp of labored effort. Marshall may have been, as Air Marshal Sir John Slessor called him, "a magnificent-looking man ... superbly confident in himself and the rightness of his opinions," but his was a countenance that resisted compelling articulation, his "heavily handsome face expressionless save for a permanent suggestion of disappointment at the world's failure to match his own Olympian qualities of mind and comportment."[6] The "veriest newsboy" might see in him the incarnation of authority, but that authority confounded common expectations of what a general ought to look like.[7] Americans had not seen many generals in the 1930s; their memories were populated with warrior heroes like Washington or Lee, Grant, Pershing, MacArthur—the only American military men of whom they retained a clear image. In Marshall, there was no visible vainglory, not attitudinizing, no bone-and-gristle ferocity. The countenance reflected the character. (At Marshall's alma mater, there are three large statues: George Washington, Stonewall Jackson, and George Marshall. Marshall's lack of pretension, the quiet functionality of his character, are in striking contrast to the sculptural depictions of his eighteenth- and nineteenth-century military forebearers).

The best of the *TIME* cover renderings is the first. It was a simple black-and-white photograph taken around the time of Marshall's appointment as chief of staff. He seems a trifle young for his station; he is slender and not yet careworn; his expression bespeaks hope as well as confidence. It is the expression an ardent young officer hopes to find on the face of his commanding general. For once he is wearing a full array of decorations, including medal ribbons for the French Légion d'honneur and the American Distinguished Service Medal. There is a little touch of elegance in a thin gold collar bar. Under the photos are the words MARSHALL: CHIEF OF STAFF. Under this, the *TIME* tagline, neither ironic nor arch: "Soldiers have always said there's no one like him."

The army of 1940, on the lip of a seismic change, was

still unto itself. *This* was the army that understood there was no one like Marshall. Harry Hopkins's counsel and John Pershing's devoted admiration (and General Hugh Drum's foolish campaigning for the chief of staff's job) powerfully influenced President Franklin Roosevelt's educated instinct in selecting Marshall, but the army had all along known that he was its summa. Whether he was a colonel or brigadier, tucked away in Chicago or in the Pacific Northwest, he remained at dead center in the conscious memories of all who had served with him or who knew of his work in France, in China, at Fort Benning.

For all the reverence that the army may have had for Marshall, he was not always an easy man to work for. There were episodes of temper—Colonel Harold Bull, later chief of operations in Europe under Dwight Eisenhower, remembered him angrily flinging a briefcase full of papers across an office. "I was never at ease when I made a presentation to him," Omar Bradley wrote.[8] These cases, however, were not all that frequent; indeed, they grew rarer as the war went on. Marshall's standards were unvaryingly high, and he had a way of communicating both disappointment and irritation, particularly over written memoranda that the secretaries of the general staff and their assistants had prepared for his signature, that kept subordinates on the qui vive. A letter drafted or a memorandum prepared that contained no criticism or rewriting by the chief was celebrated and treasured as a small trophy.

The War Department itself, as the coming of war made plain, was in Marshall's words, "the poorest command post in the Army."[9] Barely three months after Pearl Harbor, Marshall would make it an extraordinarily efficient instrumentality for the management of America's global war, but until then, army headquarters subsisted as sclerotic congeries of superannuated bureaus, departments, semi-independent agencies, and offices "as jealous of their privileges as a clutch of feudal barons."[10] Marshall's official biographer presented a striking example of its operation, quoting General Joseph McNarney, deputy chief of staff, who would be in charge of implementing this reorganization:

> If a decision had to be made that affected an individual doughboy it had to be referred over to the Chief of Infantry [to] get his recommendation on it, and [then] back to the General Staff section; it went up to one of the Secretaries, General Staff, and they had at least eight assistant secretaries ... who did nothing but brief papers so that they could be presented to the Chief of Staff.[11]

Marshall called McNarney a merciless man. With General Henry Arnold, deputy for air, and with Marshall's full backing, they carried through a root-and-branch reorganization in March 1942 and allowed senior officers whose positions were being eliminated little time to protest. Marshall backed McNarney ruthlessly.

He had told him that getting a paper through the War Department bureaucracy, through a process called "concurrences," was ridiculous: "About twenty-eight people had to pass on matters. I can't stand it."[12]

Some sixty-one officers answered directly to the chief of staff; 30 major and 350 smaller commands were directly responsible to him. It is a measure of the president's confidence in Marshall (and the secretary of war's enthusiastic endorsement of the reorganization) that the process was carried through in less than a month. Under the new system, only six officers would report to the chief of staff and the army would be organized under three commands: Army Ground Forces (General Lesley McNair); Army Air Forces (General Henry Arnold); Army Service Forces (Lieutenant General Brehon Somervell). Descriptions of the characters and operating qualities of these figures bristle with adjectives like "ruthless," "efficient," "uncompromising," "demanding," "drastic." The president approved the reorganization on March 9 with a wave of his hand and a vigorous assent. Contemporaries noted that the US Navy, whose own organizational practices were often obscure and Byzantine, would have been far less susceptible, given the president's lifelong interest in naval matters and his own service as assistant secretary of the navy, to such radical reorganization.

On July 1, 1941, Marshall published the first *Biennial Report of the Chief of Staff*. Its purpose was frankly polemical—it was an instrument of persuasion as much

as an assembly of information. The report is a useful
account of how the American army was transformed
from its interwar inconsequentiality into a force almost,
if not quite, ready to engage its country's enemies in
battle. Marshall considered this period, particularly the
months between May 1940 and the Japanese attack upon
Pearl Harbor, the most taxing of all his service for two
reasons: first, because his superiors—the president and
Congress—were either reluctant to appropriate the funds
necessary for the transformation of the military establishment or were uncertain as to how those funds might
usefully be committed; and second, each, and sometimes
both, seemed unwilling to make the decisions—decisions
other than financial ones—necessary to enable the chief
of staff to prepare the army for its services abroad.

·   ·   ·

The demands of Marshall's wartime duties and commitments would now come at him in full flood, in
unremitting simultaneity. To the student of his life, the
temptation to disentangle such demands and duties is
almost irresistible. Marshall was responsible for grand
strategy, organization, global command, public advocacy,
coalition politics and diplomacy, counsel to the commander in chief. Great not only in their breadth but
also their importance to the wartime effort, these duties
required the knowledge, habits of character, and sense
of leadership that Marshall had cultivated for all his

life, sometimes intentionally, but certainly not always. While many books have been written, and will continue to be written, on how Marshall approached each of his responsibilities, Marshall did not have the luxury of distinguishing one from another: he had to address and engage them all. But such was far from the ideal texture of the chief of staff's way of working, of *mastering* his responsibilities.

This is the portrait of the man who would soon help shape the course of history.

Acknowledgments

This book has been many years in the making. As does any author, I owe debts to countless individuals who have offered their friendship, advice, and feedback, without which this book would not have been possible. There are, however, a few thanks that merit particular attention here (in no particular order of importance).

First, I would like to express my thanks to Andrew Miller, my longtime editor at Knopf, who, through many hours of reading and commenting some years ago, substantially shaped the course of this project. Although a recent promotion resulted in Andrew's need to transfer his editorship to a colleague at Knopf, without his interest in this project and incisive commentary on earlier drafts, this book would not have been possible.

I would also like to express my thanks to my second editor at Knopf, Todd Portnowitz, who has expertly shepherded this book through its final stages of revision. His guidance and administrative support have been invaluable.

In the fall of 2021, I had the occasion to meet Dennis Wieboldt, then a first-year graduate student in American history at Boston College, who responded to a job posting for an editorial assistantship. Although he was a full-time student in Boston throughout much of this assistantship, he drove to my home in Newport, Rhode Island, in the wee hours of the morning and evening to facilitate the eventual publication of this book. In many ways, Dennis's advice, organization, and management in this project's final months made it possible for this book to be finished in the form that it has. And, while his sharpness of intellect and keen editorial skills enhanced the writing of this book, it is for his friendship and affectionate support that I am most grateful. In the laborious process of writing, authentic and meaningful friendships such as these are as important as any technical skill. For Dennis's willingness to offer both his skills and friendship, I express my utmost appreciation.

Finally, and most importantly, my deepest debts are owed to my wife, Diana, whose constant love has been sustaining beyond measure. In her steadfast support and compassion, she has become as responsible as I for the completion of this project.

Notes

Chapter One: My Youngest and My Last

1. Forrest C. Pogue, *George C. Marshall: Education of a General, 1880–1939* (New York: Penguin Books, 1993), 34.
2. Pogue, *Education of a General* (1993), 27.
3. Pogue, *Education of a General* (1993), 23.
4. Mary Augusta Rodgers, "Old Kentucky Towns," *New York Times,* October 5, 1986.
5. Pogue, *Education of a General* (1993), 41.
6. George C. Marshall, *Interviews and Reminiscences for Forrest C. Pogue* (Lexington, VA: George C. Marshall Research Foundation, 1991), 70.
7. *"Fully the Equal of the Best": George C. Marshall and the Virginia Military Institute* (Lexington, VA: George C. Marshall Foundation, 1996), 4–5.

Chapter Two: Marshall at VMI

1. Benjamin Franklin, *Autobiography,* ed. J. A. Leo Lemay and P. M. Zall (New York: Norton, 1985), 78–79.
2. An ironic contrast: Robert E. Lee, president of neighboring Washington College (later Washington and Lee University),

wrote in his *Personal Reminiscences* that "he did not propose to train men for the Army but for pursuits of civil life, and that in his best view the discipline fitted to make soldiers was *not* best suited to qualify young men for the duties of citizens." J. William Jones, ed., *Personal Reminiscences of General Robert E. Lee* (Baton Rouge: Louisiana State University Press, 1994), 93. First published 1874.

3. George C. Marshall, *Interviews and Reminiscences for Forrest C. Pogue* (Lexington, VA: George C. Marshall Research Foundation, 1986), 95.

4. John Sergeant Wise, *The End of an Era: The Story of a New Market Cadet* (Boston: Houghton Mifflin, 1899), 240.

5. Reproduced in George F. Will, "Marshall's Monument," *Washington Post*, June 1, 1997.

6. William Frye, *Marshall: Citizen Soldier* (Indianapolis: Bobbs-Merrill, 1947), 60–61.

7. Forrest C. Pogue, *George C. Marshall: Education of a General, 1880–1939* (New York: Penguin Books, 1993), 88.

Chapter Three: Early Service, Philippines

1. Douglas MacArthur, *Reminiscences* (Annapolis, MD: Naval Institute Press, 2001), 29. First published 1964.

2. Reproduced in Eric Grynaviski, *America's Middlemen: Power at the Edge of Empire* (Cambridge: Cambridge University Press, 2018), 192.

3. Barbara W. Tuchman, *Stilwell and the American Experience in China* (New York: Random House, 2017), 26.

4. George C. Marshall, *Interviews and Reminiscences for Forrest C. Pogue* (Lexington, VA: George C. Marshall Research Foundation, 1986), 121.

5. William Frye, *Marshall: Citizen Soldier* (Chicago: Arcole, 1947), 81.

6. Forrest C. Pogue, *George C. Marshall: Education of a General, 1880–1939* (New York: Penguin Books, 1993), 78.

7. Pogue, *Education of a General* (1993), 80.

Chapter Four: Fort Reno

1. George C. Marshall, *Interviews and Reminiscences for Forrest C. Pogue* (Lexington, VA: George C. Marshall Research Foundation, 1986), 145.

2. As noted by historian Paul Kennedy: "When the famous British warship designer Sir William White made a tour of the United States in 1904, he was shaken to discover fourteen battleships and thirteen armored cruisers being built simultaneously in American yards." Although the army was kept on starvation rations, here was a foretaste of American capacity to produce military and naval hardware when moved to do so. It was the third year of Theodore Roosevelt's presidency. Paul Kennedy, *The Rise and Fall of the Great Powers: Economic Change and Military Conflict from 1500 to 2000* (New York: Vintage Books, 1987), 243.

3. In 1953 a reporter asked George Marshall, who had just learned he had been awarded the Nobel Peace Prize, what he considered to be his most important contribution to peace: Marshall replied that it was his work in raising and training an army, and getting the country to support the effort, in 1940.

4. Reproduced in James R. Holmes, "'A Striking Thing': Leadership, Strategic Communications, and Roosevelt's Great White Fleet," *Naval War College Review* 61, no. 1 (Winter 2008): 54.

Chapter Five: Fort Leavenworth

1. George C. Marshall, *Interviews and Reminiscences for Forrest C. Pogue* (Lexington, VA: George C. Marshall Research Foundation, 1986), 96.

2. Marshall, *Interviews and Reminiscences*, 153.

3. Irving Brinton Holley, *General John M. Palmer, Citizen Soldiers, and the Army of a Democracy* (Westport, CT: Greenwood Press, 1982), 187.

4. He was promoted to first lieutenant as of March 7.

5. Forrest C. Pogue, *George C. Marshall: Education of a General, 1880–1939* (New York: Penguin Books, 1993), 122.

6. Holley, *General John M. Palmer,* 183.

7. Holley, *General John M. Palmer,* 183.

Chapter Six: Lieutenant and Captain

1. Forrest C. Pogue, *George C. Marshall: Education of a General, 1880–1939* (New York: Penguin Books, 1993), 123.

2. Larry I. Bland and Sharon R. Ritenour, eds., *The Papers of George Catlett Marshall,* vol. 1 (Baltimore, MD: Johns Hopkins University Press), 84. (Emphasis added.)

3. Mark A. Stoler, *George C. Marshall: Soldier-Statesman of the American Century* (Boston: Twayne, 1989), 29.

4. Russell F. Weigley, *History of the United States Army* (New York: Macmillan, 1967), 568.

5. Pogue, *Education of a General* (1993), 136.

6. Pogue, *Education of a General* (1993), 137–38.

7. Pogue, *Education of a General* (1993), 138.

8. Pogue, *Education of a General* (1993), 138.

9. Bell had "grippe" (influenza) and, as a candidate for a command in France, wished to hide any evidence of physical frailty. He was sixty-two.

10. Quoted in *The Writings of George Washington; Being His Correspondence, Addresses, Messages, and Other Papers, Official and Private,* ed. Jared Sparks, vol. 3 (Boston: Russel, Odiorne, and Metcalf; and Hillary, Gray, and Co., 1834), 116, 258.

11. Pogue, *Education of a General* (1993), 143.

Chapter Seven: First World War

1. Richard Eberhart, "The Fury of Aerial Bombardment," https://allpoetry.com.

2. George C. Marshall, *Interviews and Reminiscences for Forrest C. Pogue* (Lexington, VA: George C. Marshall Research Foundation, 1986), 191.

3. Rather than commenting on the weather with the phrase *Il fait*

très beau aujourd'hui ("It's very nice out today"), Marshall paid himself a compliment ("I am very beautiful today").

4. Martin Gilbert, *The First World War: A Complete History* (New York: Henry Holt, 1994), 414; Vera Brittain, *Testament of Youth: An Autobiographical Study of the Years 1900–1925* (New York: Penguin Classics, 2005).

5. Pershing to Col. Dennis Nolan (September 13, 1918) in Donald Smythe, *Pershing: General of the Armies,* vol. 2 (Bloomington: Indiana University Press, 1986), 187; quoted in Leif A. Torkelsen, "'Battles Were Not Fought In Lines': Nationalism, Industrialism and Progressivism in the American Military Discourse, 1865–1918" (PhD dissertation, The Ohio State University, 2018), 174.

6. Forrest C. Pogue, *George C. Marshall: Education of a General, 1880–1939* (New York: Penguin Books, 1993), 148.

7. Pogue, *Education of a General* (1993), 148.

8. Eric Larrabee, *Commander in Chief: Franklin Delano Roosevelt, His Lieutenants, and Their War* (New York: Simon & Schuster, 1987), 487.

9. Edward M. Coffman, *The War to End All Wars: The American Military Experience in World War I* (Madison: University of Wisconsin Press, 1986), 133.

10. Marshall, *Memoirs,* 49.

11. Forrest C. Pogue, *George C. Marshall: Education of a General, 1880–1939* (New York: Viking, 1963), 153.

12. S. L. A. Marshall, *The American Heritage History of World War I* (New York: Houghton Mifflin, 1964), 279.

13. Russell F. Weigley, *History of the United States Army* (New York: Macmillan, 1967), 381.

14. George C. Marshall, *Memoirs of My Services in the World War, 1917–1918* (New York: Houghton Mifflin, 1976), 52.

15. Larry I. Bland and Sharon R. Ritenour, eds., *The Papers of George Catlett Marshall,* vol. 1 (Baltimore, MD: Johns Hopkins University Press), 134.

16. Bland and Ritenour, *Papers,* 134.

17. Ed Cray, *General of the Army: George C. Marshall, Soldier and Statesman* (New York: Cooper Square Press, 2000), 61.

18. Pogue, *Education of a General* (1963), 165.

19. Pogue, *Education of a General* (1963), 168.

20. Bland and Ritenour, *Papers*, 143.

21. Kenneth S. Davis, *FDR: Into the Storm, 1937–1940: A History* (New York: Random House, 1993), 382.

22. Marshall, *Memoirs*, 116.

23. Marshall, *Memoirs*, 117.

24. Marshall, *Memoirs*, 117.

25. Marshall, *Memoirs*, 120.

26. Marshall, *Memoirs*, 121.

27. Marshall, *Memoirs*, 123.

28. Marshall, *Memoirs*, 125.

29. Marshall, *Interviews and Reminiscences*, 220.

30. Gary Mead, *The Doughboys: America and the First World War* (London: Overlook Books, 2000), 286.

31. Marshall, *Memoirs*, 137.

32. Marshall, *Memoirs*, 139.

33. A copy of this plan, in a crushed mimeograph left in a Belfort Hotel wastebasket, would serve the same function as Eisenhower's "Fortitude" deception in June 1944—that is, persuading the enemy *not* to reinforce other fronts under actual attack.

34. Marshall, *Memoirs*, 139.

35. Pogue, *Education of a General* (1993), 176.

36. Richard Slotkin, *Lost Battalions: The Great War and the Crisis of American Nationality* (New York: Henry Holt, 2005), 245.

37. Slotkin, *Lost Battalions*, 272.

38. Marshall mentioned US casualties of 176,000 wounded or sick requiring evacuation—the "sick" mainly sufferers from influenza.

39. Pogue, *Education of a General* (1993), 184.

40. Pogue, *Education of a General* (1993), 184.

41. Marshall, *Memoirs*, 189–92.

Chapter Eight: Between the Two World Wars

1. Forrest C. Pogue, *George C. Marshall: Education of a General, 1880–1939* (New York: Penguin Books, 1993), 190.

2. Quoted in Blaine A. Horton, "A Most Efficient Officer in Every Respect," unpublished paper, 80.

3. $30,000 in 1919 being worth at least a half million dollars in 2008 values.

4. Mark Twain, "Chapters from My Autobiography—XII," *North American Review* 184, no. 609 (February 1907): 345, http://www.jstor.org/stable/25105789.

5. Marshall, *Memoirs*, 214.

6. Marshall, *Memoirs*, 214. (Emphasis added.)

7. Marshall, *Memoirs*, 214.

8. Marshall, *Memoirs*, 214.

9. Marshall, *Memoirs*, 223.

10. Russell F. Weigley, *History of the United States Army* (New York: Macmillan, 1967), 396.

11. Edward M. Coffman, *The Regulars: The American Army, 1898–1941* (Cambridge, MA: Harvard University Press, 2004), 232.

12. Pogue, *Education of a General* (1993), 225–26.

13. Weigley, *History*, 394.

14. Reproduced in Allan Carlson, "Your Honey or Your Life: The Case for the Bachelor Army," *Policy Review* 66 (Fall 1993).

15. Larry I. Bland and Sharon R. Ritenour, eds., *The Papers of George Catlett Marshall*, vol. 1 (Baltimore, MD: Johns Hopkins University Press), 202–3.

16. George C. Marshall, "Profiting by War Experiences," *Infantry Journal* 18 (January 1921): 37.

17. William Frye, *Marshall: Citizen Soldier* (Chicago: Arcole, 1947), 181.

Chapter Nine: China

1. David M. Kennedy, *Freedom from Fear: The American People in Depression and War, 1929–1945* (New York: Oxford University Press, 1999), 430.

2. Forrest C. Pogue, *George C. Marshall: Education of a General, 1880–1939* (New York: Penguin Books, 1993), 243. Impossible in 1925, it remained so in 1946.

3. Larry I. Bland and Sharon R. Ritenour, eds., *The Papers of George Catlett Marshall*, vol. 1 (Baltimore, MD: Johns Hopkins University Press), 298.

4. Bland and Ritenour, *Papers,* 309.

Chapter Ten: Teacher

1. Reproduced in Richard G. Weingardt, "Robert E. Lee: Larger-Than-Life Icon," *Leadership and Management in Engineering* (July 2013): 215.

2. Much later Marshall had to be persuaded to abandon his bias against Captain James A. Van Fleet, American Eighth Army commander in Korea in succession to Matthew Ridgway. Marshall had mixed his name up with another officer of the same surname who was a drunk.

3. United States Infantry School, *Infantry in Battle* (Washington, DC: Infantry Journal, 1939), 1.

4. Discussed in Eric Niderost, "Grant's Ordeal at the Battle of Shiloh," *Military Heritage* 20, no. 5 (March 2019).

Chapter Eleven: Fort Screven and Vancouver Barracks

1. Forrest C. Pogue, *George C. Marshall: Education of a General, 1880–1939* (New York: Penguin Books, 1993), 274.

2. Pogue, *Education of a General* (1993), 392.

3. Pogue, *Education of a General* (1993), 393.

4. *Savannah Morning News,* April 23, 1978.

5. Discussed in Stanley Weintraub, "Marshall & MacArthur: Tortoise and the Hare," HistoryNet.com, October 1, 2018.

6. Larry I. Bland and Sharon R. Ritenour, eds., *The Papers of George Catlett Marshall*, vol. 1 (Baltimore, MD: Johns Hopkins University Press), 484.

7. Bland and Ritenour, *Papers,* 462.

8. Bland and Ritenour, *Papers,* 408.

9. Marshall to Edwin F. Harding, October 31, 1934 (#1–358),

George C. Marshall Papers, Illinois National Guard, George C. Marshall Research Library, Lexington, Virginia.

10. The position's term was four years.

11. Bland and Ritenour, *Papers,* 508.

Chapter Twelve: Conclusion: A Soldier for Democracy

1. David Hackett Fischer, *Washington's Crossing* (New York: Oxford University Press, 2004), 12.

2. Fischer, *Washington's Crossing,* 13.

3. One of Marshall's finest appointments was a woman, Oveta Culp Hobby, to lead the Women's Army Corps.

4. George C. Marshall, *Interviews and Reminiscences for Forrest C. Pogue* (Lexington, VA: George C. Marshall Research Foundation, 1986), 203.

5. Isaiah Berlin, *Personal Impressions,* ed. Henry Hardy (New York: Viking, 1981), 12.

6. Eric Larrabee, *Commander in Chief: Franklin Delano Roosevelt, His Lieutenants, and Their War* (New York: Simon & Schuster, 1987), 99; John Keegan, *Six Armies in Normandy: From D-Day to the Liberation of Paris* (New York: Penguin, 1982), 43.

7. Larrabee, *Commander in Chief,* 98.

8. Omar Bradley and Clay Blair, *A General's Life: An Autobiography* (New York: Simon & Schuster, 1983), 83.

9. Ray S. Cline, *Washington Command Post: The Operations Division* (Washington, DC: Office of the Chief of Military History, Dept. of the Army, 1951), 72.

10. Forrest Pogue, *George C. Marshall: Ordeal and Hope, 1939–1942* (New York: Viking, 1965), 290.

11. Pogue, *Ordeal and Hope,* 290.

12. Pogue, *Ordeal and Hope,* 293.

Index

A NOTE ABOUT THE AUTHOR

Josiah Bunting III is an author, educator, and military historian. A graduate of the Virginia Military Institute and former Rhodes Scholar at the University of Oxford, he served as a major in the United States Army and later as the superintendent of the Virginia Military Institute. His previous books include *The Lionheads* (one of *TIME*'s Ten Best Novels of 1973) and *Ulysses S. Grant* (published as part of Arthur M. Schlesinger Jr.'s American Presidents series). In recognition of his many accomplishments and lifelong devotion to higher education, Bunting was appointed to the National Council of the National Endowment for the Humanities by President George W. Bush. He lives with his wife in Newport, Rhode Island.

A NOTE ON THE TYPE

This book was set in a modern adaptation of a type designed by the first William Caslon (1692–1766). The Caslon face, an artistic, easily read type, has enjoyed more than two centuries of popularity in the English-speaking world. This version, with its even balance and honest letterforms, was designed by Carol Twombly for the Adobe Corporation and released in 1990.

Composed by North Market Street Graphics
Lancaster, Pennsylvania

Printed and bound by Berryville Graphics
Berryville, Virginia

Designed by Michael Collica